Contents

Introduction

Essay Questions: Communist Russia

Contents

Documents: Source-Based Exercises

Examination board sources

These exam-length answers to essay and document questions are based on Special Subject papers set by the following examination boards. They are divided into Main and Subsidiary sections according to the number of Essay/Document questions in the paper.

They will also be useful to those studying (1) European Outlines papers of the 20th century and (2) suitable papers set at A/S-level.

Fascist Italy

Main:

London, Papers 8 and 14, The Dictatorships in Europe, 1919–39
NEAB, Alternative E, Rivalry & Conflict in Europe, 1870–1939

Subsidiary:

Cambridge, Paper 21, The Origins of the Second World War, 1929–39

Communist Russia

Main:

London, Papers 8 and 14 (as above)
London, Syllabus D, International Problems since 1921
O and C, Papers 31 and 43, Russia in Revolution, 1905–21
Cambridge, Paper 20/21, The Origins of the Second World War, 1929–39
NEAB, Alternative E (as above)
AEB, 0630, Option 08, The Russian Revolution, 1914–1933

Subsidiary:

Cambridge, Document-Based Topics (9020/13) Hitler & Germany

Nazi Germany

Main:

London, Papers 8 and 14 (as above)
NEAB, Alternative E (as above)
AEB, 0630, Option 09, National Socialist Germany, 1933–45
O and C, Papers 32 and 44, The Rise of Hitler and the Third Reich
Oxford, Unit 1, 18, The Rise of Hitler and the Impact of Nazi Rule on German Government & Society, 1928–39
Oxford, Unit 4, Topic area 8, 9, 10
Oxford, Unit 5, Topic 5

Subsidiary:

Cambridge, Document-Based Topics (9020/13) Hitler & Germany, 1933–45
Cambridge, Paper 21 (as above)

We gratefully acknowledge permission from the Oxford and Cambridge Schools Examinations Board and the University of London Examinations and Assessment Council to reproduce document questions from their past examination papers. The Oxford and Cambridge Examinations Board and the University of London Examinations and Assessment Council accept no responsibility whatsoever for the accuracy or method of working in the answers given.

Introduction

The object of this book is to help the student of AS/A-level European History to acquire suitable techniques for answering essay and document questions. 'Fine!' you may say, 'but how can you do that?' The answer is, of course, that it's you, the student, who's going to do it. I shall provide in this introduction an outline of the rules which will lead to better essays. Some, perhaps all, you may be familiar with; I beg you to give the others a trial.

The specimen essays which follow do obey these rules, so you can see them put into practice. In the notes which accompany the essays, you'll find much that should be helpful for your essay writing in an AS/A-level exam. They will analyse the question, comment on the structure of the essay and its content, advise you of common pitfalls to be wary of and provide you with further questions on the same topic so that you can think flexibly around it and practise the skills you have learnt.

But don't think of these essays as 'model answers'. There is no point in learning them by heart in the vain hope that an exactly similar question will appear in your exam; rather, they should provide you with factual content for key topics, examples of correct essay technique and the means to further practice which will improve your own exam answers.

In addition to the essays, I've provided ten document exercises. Some suggestions for answering these are given in this introduction; the answers are commented on in the same way as the essays.

The writing of exam-length answers and the answering of source-based questions at A-level are both techniques which candidates will need to master before facing the examiners. As in learning any technique, practice is vital, and the 'weekly essay' and answers to past source-based questions will provide this. The various hints offered below – in question-and-answer mode – may help candidates to write better answers, but provide no magic road to a good grade. Nor will the learning of specimen essays or document answers – unless you're fortunate enough to discover an exactly similar question in a future paper! What you may hope to learn is something of the correct technique, and some useful factual information, which may be employed in answering similar questions in the future.

Question 1: 'I am getting reasonable grades in my weekly essays. How different are exam answers?'

Answer: The most obvious difference is in the time available – 40 minutes in most exam papers as against the 7 days that you should have to write your weekly essay (even though it may be done the night before it is due in!). The essays in this book are 900–950 words long – about the maximum that can be written in 40–45 minutes. When you begin to write A-level examination answers, you'll find it hard to write as much as this: at the end of your two-year course, you should be doing so regularly.

Question 2: 'But surely quality is more important than quantity in an exam answer?'

Answer: True, but you should find, as you become more experienced, that you'll need to write at the length I've suggested, if you're to answer the question in full. This does not mean padding out your answer with 'waffle' (remember that examiners are busy people), but it does mean answering all aspects of the question and including sufficient relevant factual detail.

Question 3:   'So how do I plan my answer to make sure it's the right length?'

Answer: Obviously, you'll not have the time to make the elaborate plan which you may (I hope) have used in your longer essays. You must also be familiar with the rules of your Examining Board as to how, and if, essay plans should be included on your paper.

You'll need a **mini essay plan (MEP)** which will contain three essential parts: (1) an indication of the *number of paragraphs* you'll use; (2) *a title for each paragraph*; (3) a *clear answer* to the question (in one or two sentences). This is a minimum: you can write more under each paragraph heading and give more detail in the conclusion (as in the essay plans at the end of each essay answer in this book).

From this, the examiners will be able to see how you're proposing to tackle the question and what your answer will be. Should you not finish writing your answer for any reason, they will be able to give you credit for what you intended to write. Above all, it will provide a plan for your answer which should guarantee that it is relevant to the question. But make sure that you write the same number of paragraphs, and come to the same conclusion, as in your plan!

Question 4:   'I often find that I'm writing a lot of short paragraphs in my answer, particularly when I'm running out of time. How many paragraphs should I use?'

Answer: Make it a rule that you never, in an exam, write more than **six paragraphs**, plus an **introduction** and a **conclusion**. None of the essay answers in this book contains more than eight paragraphs; I can assure you that *any* A-level question can be answered correctly in this number of paragraphs. If you find yourself using a lot of short paragraphs towards the end of an essay answer, it is unlikely that they will correspond with any reliable essay plan; more likely, you'll have abandoned your plan – or, perhaps, you never had one?

Question 5:   'I can see that paragraphs are important in my answer. Why is this?'

Answer: Paragraphs are the 'essential building blocks' of an essay. If you use them correctly, you can actually convey to the examiner more than is contained in the paragraph itself. Whenever you allot a paragraph to a particular part of your argument, you're telling the examiners that they may assume that the point you're making is of equal importance to the other paragraphs in your answer. They may be of very different lengths, but by using them you've shown that the points they cover are of equal importance. In an extreme example, you might write a paragraph of one sentence; by doing so, you're indicating that this sentence is of equal importance to another paragraph of, say, ten sentences.

Question 6:   'So I obviously need to write good paragraphs. What should they be like?'

Answer: Don't make them too long; put them in 'reader friendly' *order* in your answer; if you can, make the answer '*flow*' by using the last sentence of one paragraph to 'link' with the first sentence of the next; write a clear **topic sentence** (which will already have been indicated in your **mini essay plan**), describing the main purpose of the paragraph in your line of argument; where possible, put the topic sentence *first*.

Question 7: 'I often find it difficult to write the first sentence of an essay answer. How should I begin?'

Answer: This brings us on to **introductions**. Here is a useful rule which should help you to get going. Introductions should do three things: (1) *assess* the question, showing that you fully understand its implications; (2) *define* any words used in the question the meaning of which may be at all doubtful; (3) *indicate* the line of argument by which you'll attempt to answer the question – as already shown in your mini essay plan. I've tried to follow these rules in writing the introductions to the essays in this book.

You may object that (3) is repetitious, but it's vitally important to get the plan of your answer into your own head and to indicate it to the examiners. Always remember that the most common complaint in Examiners' Reports is that candidates fail to answer the question.

Question 8: 'Can you give me some similar advice to help me finish off my answer?'

Answer: The writing of **conclusions** is less easy to reduce to a set of rules. The following may help:

(a) Essentials:
    (i)   Try to *repeat the question* – not necessarily in the same words – to re-focus the attention of the reader (and *yourself*) upon it.
    (ii) Provide a clear *answer* to the question (or to each part of the question).
    (iii) Possibly use a *quotation* as your final sentence.

(b) Do:
    (i)   make sure you put in a **conclusion** (and that it is the same as that in your plan; if you change your mind about your conclusion while you're writing the essay, then *alter your plan*).
    (ii) answer each part of a multi-part question.

(c) Don't:
    (i)   answer another question which you would have preferred the examiner to ask.
    (ii) include *new* points of argument, which you haven't discussed in your essay, in your conclusion.
    (iii) waste time trying to think of a brilliant final sentence.

Question 9: 'People often criticise my spelling, grammar and punctuation. Have you any useful tips?'

Answer: **(a) Spelling**
Make sure that you spell any words on the question paper correctly; **learn** the correct spelling of important names, places, etc. in your syllabus; **don't** get too worried about spelling – it's more important for you to write clear, grammatical sentences than that every word in them should be correctly spelt.

(b) Grammar/Syntax
The examiners cannot give you credit for anything they cannot understand. Therefore write in *short sentences*, unless you can handle longer ones. Learn how to punctuate (see below); *don't* use contractions (isn't, can't); *do* avoid most abbreviations, the use of the first person ('I') and all jargon, cliché, vogue words and slang.

(c) Punctuation

You can write a perfectly clear and acceptable essay answer using nothing but commas and full-stops. But the semi-colon is useful in dividing short sentences with a common theme, and the colon, followed by semi-colons or commas, is invaluable for introducing lists. There are many examples of both in this book.

Learn the rules for punctuating and incorporating quotations in your answers and the proper use of the apostrophe.

Question 10: 'All this should help me to write better answers, but I often have difficulty in understanding the question.'

Answer: The analysis of questions, however you do it, is vital for a successful answer. Some people suggest dividing all questions into **three** parts, but it may be simpler to distinguish **two**. These are: (1) **instruction** and (2) **topic/focus**.

The **instruction** part of the question indicates whether **explanation** (why...?; account for...; examine the role of... etc.) or **assessment/evaluation** (to what extent...?; how successful...?; evaluate the... etc.) is required.

For example:

(a) 'Account for the victory of the Bolsheviks in the civil war.' (explanation)

(b) 'How totalitarian was Mussolini's rule in Italy?' (assessment)

(c) 'What problems faced Hitler as Chancellor in January 1933, and how far had they been solved by the end of the following year?' (a combination of both types – explanation and assessment).

The **topic/focus** part of the question shows what topic the question is concerned with and how the answer must be focused on that topic. Thus in (a) above, the topic is the civil war and the answer must be focused on the victory of the Bolsheviks; in (b), the topic is Mussolini and the focus is on the totalitarian nature of his rule in Italy; similarly in (c), the topic is Germany, from January 1933 to the end of 1944, and the focus is on Hitler's problems as Chancellor and his success in solving them.

Question 11: 'What else can be done to analyse the question?'

Answer: Plenty!

(a) Consider whether you're dealing with a short or long question. (Long questions are easier; they provide more information.)

(b) Decide whether it's a *'relative importance'* question. Consider the question: 'Would you agree that World War Two was "Hitler's War"?' In your answer, you must balance all the causes of World War Two against Hitler being the chief cause.

(c) What about questions containing a quotation? In these you should note the following:

  (i) You must take careful note of the *instruction*. If you're asked to *'discuss'*, you must say whether you *agree, disagree* or *partially agree* with the statement made in the quotation.

  (ii) You should weigh up the arguments and evidence for and against what is stated in the quotation and say, in your conclusion, what view you support and why.

  (iii) Note that you can agree with one part of the quotation and not another.

(d) *Discussion questions.* These require you to provide arguments for and against a statement and to give your own conclusion. Consider the following questions:

4

(i) 'The Provisional Government was doomed to failure because its authority was nominal rather than real.' Discuss.

(ii) How far do you see Hitler as a 'weak dictator' in his command of domestic policy in the Third Reich?

Both these questions require you to give arguments for and against when discussing the truth of the statement in the question plus, of course, your own opinion. In Essay 3, that opinion is that there is a more important reason for the failure of the Provisional Government.

(e) *Compare and contrast questions.* These are not so common in history papers as in some other subjects; should you meet one, such as: 'Compare and contrast the aims of the Bolsheviks and other opposition groups in Russia in 1917', you should decide the aims you're going to consider and then write one or two paragraphs on each, *comparing similarities and contrasting differences* for the various parties you have chosen to consider.

(f) *'To what extent...?','How far...?','How true is it to say...?' questions.* For example: 'How totalitarian was Mussolini's rule in Italy?' The answer is invariably 'to some extent' and the plan should include some statement of the case 'for' and of the case 'against' with a *conclusion* which can include the phrase 'It is true to the extent that... but not to the extent that...'.

Question 12: 'How are answers to document questions different from those for essay questions?'

Answer: Many of the same rules apply. Express yourself clearly, answer the question, use paragraphs to show the relative importance of points in your argument. Carefully work out the time you can spend on a document question, as compared to your timing on an essay question, in a paper which contains both. Remember that it can be easier to score high marks in answering the former than the latter. Write answers of sufficient length (the maximum marks for each question given on the paper will help you here) and try to find all the clues in the evidence presented to you, while watching the time you spend on each part of the question and making sure that you finish all the parts, particularly the last, which is often worth the most marks. Remember that some of the questions will require no more than an accurate and detailed *comprehension* of the sources; others will ask you to *evaluate* their reliability; still others will require *comparison* of different sources. Careful reading of the question is, as always, essential. *Distinguish between* (a) those questions which ask you to 'use the evidence of the sources alone' and (b) those which allow you to use your own knowledge as well as the evidence in the sources (I suggest that you might write this type of answer in *two* paragraphs: one for the evidence provided by the sources and one for evidence from your own knowledge). Use the same material as in your essay paragraphs, as I've done in one or two cases.

Finally, beware of the *selective nature* of primary sources; the *motives* of those who provide them; the *bias*, conscious or unconscious, of their author. Be careful about the relationship of the *particular to the general* (e.g. how typical was one German's experiences in one area of Germany in a particular year?) and be careful of the danger of assuming knowledge that would not have been available to the author at the time. The details given about the source, particularly its date, may often be of great help in discovering the answer to a question.

Above all, remember that the document(s) given in the question are full of clues to the answers expected; as you read them through, try to note as many of these clues as possible.

How to Revise

What is revision? A definition is always useful: *revision aims to create a permanent store of information in the mind which can be used effectively in a future examination.*

How does that sound? Note that 'permanent' means, technically speaking, in your long-term memory; note also that 'can be used effectively' means that it's subject to recall and is in a form which is suitable for writing exam answers.

For many people, revision conjures up a picture of a bored student, sitting in front of a textbook, reading it in a desultory fashion and becoming more panic-stricken as the exam draws near. *This could not be more wrong!*

- Revision must not be boring; it must be *active, critical and carefully planned.*
- Revision should rely very little on textbooks and much more on *notes, essay plans and questions set in past papers.*
- A revision session should never consist only of reading; it should always contain some writing in order to be *active.*
- Above all, successful revision aims at removing much of the worry associated with exams. Candidates who have revised properly should enter the exam room *confident that they can perform to the best of their ability.*

What can we substitute for the traditional picture of the bored, passive and increasingly anxious candidate?

Remember that **time is the most precious commodity in your revision!** It is therefore essential to approach revision in a systematic way. You can do this by dividing it into **three stages**:

- **reorganisation** of notes, essays, etc.
- **redeployment** of your material to make it suitable for answering exam questions
- **recall** – practice in the ability to recall information to mind when required

So that you can have time to complete these three stages for more than one subject, you must adopt a strict **revision timetable**. Some hints on this:

- First, make sure of the **dates** of **all** your exam papers.
- Once you have drawn up your timetable, you must stick to it, but be prepared to change it if it's not working.
- **Timing**: I suggest small packets of uninterrupted study (say 20–30 minutes) followed by five-minute breaks. The morning is usually best for working – use it for your most demanding revision periods; don't try to fill too much of the timetable, but leave room for relaxation, particularly *exercise.*
- **Conditions**: Some people like absolute quiet; others prefer soft background music. Don't try to revise in competition with TV or a nearby interesting conversation involving others. Most people work best sitting at a desk rather than lolling on a sofa or a bed.
- Finally, *redraft your timetable* once the exams have begun to take account of the various papers you'll be attempting. Last-minute revision can be very important, but it must be of the right type.

Reorganisation

What does this mean? It means reorganising your notes, essays, handouts, etc. into new, concise, combined, often diagrammatic form. You've a lot of information in that bulging file you've been carrying around for the last two years, but it needs some treatment before it can be really useful for revision. We're going to give it that treatment.

What have you got? Most people will have **notes**, made from lectures by your teacher, from films, TV or radio, or from books; **essays**, written in your own time or as 'timed essays' written in class; **exam papers**, written in end-of-term or 'mock' exams; **handouts**, provided by your teacher during the course, perhaps including typed notes. **You've also now got this book!**

How do you tackle this mass of information? The answer is to divide your **reorganisation** into stages.

Stage 1: Find out what you have got

Arrange your notes into topics. These will probably be based on the weekly essays you wrote throughout the time you were preparing for the examination. Discard any topic that you didn't complete (possibly because you were ill?); it's almost certainly not worth attempting it now.

Stage 2: Shorten and combine your notes on each topic

Linear notes

As you read your notes through, add queries in the right-hand margin (if you've not got one, use the blank facing page or insert a new sheet to provide one). Don't forget to provide the answers to these queries when you've discovered them! Margins should also be used for cross-referencing other notes, essays, etc.; adding page references for definitions; even correcting spelling mistakes.

Essays

Remember that essays are a flawed answer to one question. They may be marred by errors in structure, argument, information. It's usually best to reduce them to an essay plan, with any weaknesses corrected; the most valuable thing to save may be your teacher's comments!

Exam papers

The best answers should be turned into essay plans. Teacher's comments and any notes made when the papers were gone through should be retained.

Handouts

Normally well worth keeping; they might be made into **diagrams, as could other factual material**.

Stage 3: Select your subject revision topics

Say that you're required to write a paper in which you must attempt **four** questions in three hours. When checking your notes, you find that you've covered **sixteen** topics during your course. These topics will have been chosen by your teacher to cover the syllabus, and probably also because they're popular subjects with examiners.

You may, of course, in addition to essay answers, be faced with other shorter answers by means of which the examiners can discover whether you've covered the whole syllabus. Or you may have to answer one or more *document questions* rather than some of the essay questions.

You'll not have time to cover all sixteen topics equally and it would be hard to recall everything accurately from such a mass of information. **It will therefore be necessary to choose certain topics** on which to concentrate your revision. Factors which should be taken into account when you choose your revision topics are:

(i) Which are the most popular subjects appearing in past papers? Analyse past papers and consult your teachers to discover this.

(ii) How many topics shall I revise? Say your paper requires you to answer **four** questions (from, perhaps, **twelve** or many more in an 'Outlines' paper), then the **minimum number** is $4 \times 2 = 8$. It would be safer to add two more, making a total of **ten**. Check this with past papers when you have chosen your ten topics, making sure that you've at least **six** possible questions to answer in each paper (you need more than four in case a 'topic question' is 'slanted' in a new or difficult way).

(iii) Which topics shall I revise? Considerable help on this is given in the comment on related questions in the specimen essays. Obviously, you should think carefully about choosing a topic on which you have little information (now isn't the time to embark on fresh reading); those topics which interest you most will help to motivate your revision.

But don't 'question spot' – or, in this case, 'topic spot'. You must search out the more popular topics (those that appear regularly in past papers) rather than select a topic because it hasn't appeared for a long time – it's quite possible that it won't appear this time. Nor should you try to forecast particular questions within a topic.

When you have chosen your *revision topics*, concentrate on them and don't concern yourself with those you're not covering. This is sometimes difficult to do as the exam approaches and you become worried that you haven't covered enough topics. If you've selected the topics in the way I've recommended above, you'll be quite safe; checking past papers will reinforce your decision and cheer you up!

Redeployment

It sounds a bit grand, doesn't it? What does it mean? Only that you need to get the mass of material which you have for each of your chosen revision topics into the form which will be most useful in answering the questions normally set on that topic.

What sort of form is most useful? The answer, as you may be able to guess if you've read this book, is in the form of **essay plans**.

How can you convert the material into **essay plans**? By asking **two different types of question** as you go through it.

The first type of question to be asked is that which adds to and explains the material you have. As you read through it, you should be constantly asking yourself questions: Why did that happen? Who was that man? When was that law passed? What was the result of that treaty? Who did something very similar? etc. What is more important, **you should be entering the answers to these questions in your right-hand margin or on a new left-hand page** (see above, Reorganisation, Stage 2, linear notes). In doing this, you'll be carrying out active revision, increasing the value of your notes, etc., and helping to put these facts and ideas into your long-term memory.

The **second** type of question to be asked is how to build up **essay plans** to answer the typical questions which are asked on each topic. **This is where this book will help you!**

The best way to use this book is to begin by reading it straight through. If you haven't time to do that, you should at least read through the introduction and the marginal notes which accompany each essay, paying particular attention to the sections headed *tackling the question*, *related questions* and *general comments*. You'll then have a good idea of how to:

- **analyse questions**
- **construct mini essay plans (MEPs)**
- **build answers to related questions**
- **judge the suitability of revision topics**

Remember that you'll normally have to analyse more than three related questions which you'll have obtained from past papers, textbooks, etc. Once you've done so, you should find that some of the **paragraphs** which you're using to construct **MEPs** will appear in several different answers. If you're lucky, most of the paragraphs in the *specimen essay(s)* on your topic can be used in other **MEPs**. This means that you'll need to concentrate on fewer paragraphs.

As an example of this process, look at the *related questions* at the end of *Essay 1*. *Questions 1 and 2* are the same question, put in different words, both of the *relative importance* type, and requiring you *(a)* to examine the importance of World War One as a cause of the February Revolution and *(b)* to describe any other causes of the revolution and to compare their importance with that of the war. Similarly, *Question 3* puts the chaos and incompetence of tsarist government as the stated cause of the revolution.

If we now look at the *MEP* at the end of the *specimen essay*, we see that *paragraphs 2–5* cover the importance of World War One as a possible cause of the February Revolution. In these questions, we could amalgamate *paragraphs 2 and 3* into one paragraph; we are therefore left with three more possible paragraphs in which to explore other reasons for the revolution.

In *Question 3*, the chaos and incompetence of tsarist government during the war is covered by these same paragraphs, again leaving three paragraphs to consider other causes of the 'downfall of tsardom'.

Now turn to *Essay 2* and its *related questions*. In the *specimen essay*, the personal weakness of the tsar *(paragraph 2)* provides one of the alternative reasons for the success of the revolution which we require to answer *Questions 1, 2 and 3 above*. *Paragraph 3* suggests another in the lack of co-operation with the middle classes; *paragraph 5* stresses the strength of the opposition; *paragraph 7* gives reasons for success in the events of the revolution. Thus answers to all three of the *related questions* in *Essay 1* could be written using only the paragraphs in *specimen essays 1 and 2*.

In the *related questions* to *Essay 2*, *Questions 2 and 3* are *relative importance* questions with 'the character and personality of Nicholas II' and 'the attitude of the Russian armed forces' as the stated causes of the revolution. Taking paragraphs from both *specimen essays* provides plenty of material for an *MEP* for either of these questions.

We are left with *Question 1*. This is the only question which isn't obviously of the *relative importance* type, but it's clear that the reasons for the 'little effort to save tsardom' are much the same as those that caused the revolution. By changing a few words to take account of the different slant of the question, it's quite possible to use the paragraphs in the *specimen essays* to answer it.

If we assume that you've chosen the February Revolution as one of your *revision topics*, it's now clear that the two *specimen essays* provide all that is required to answer six questions on the causes and events of that revolution. These are the most likely questions on this topic; those on its results can probably be answered by using the material in *Essay 3*.

How will you record this new information? *Essay plans* may be made in **linear** form, but diagrammatic methods may be more useful (see pages 11–13). You can use both types of **circular notes**; many people prefer **mind maps**. Paragraphs may also be recorded in **linear note-form**, or in simple **circular diagrams**.

When you have completed **'redeployment'** on all your **revision topics**, you'll be left with your notes (with cross-references and answers to the questions you've posed), plus a number of *essay plans*, in linear or diagrammatic form, to answer those questions you've selected on the various *revision topics* you've chosen.

It's now necessary to move on to the **third stage** of the *revision process*, the practice of recall, remembering that this stage should be as **active** as the other two.

Recall

You're now committing your material to your long-term memory, so that you can produce the details, as required, in the exam room. Whatever advice is offered to make this process easier, there can be no getting away from the fact that the revision of your A-level syllabus will always entail a lot of hard work. Any revision course can only offer suggestions as to how a candidate's time might be well spent; the amount of time and its quality are your own responsibility.

That said, the good news is that if the first two stages of the revision process have been completed as recommended, then much useful information will already be established in your long-term memory. The object of the recall stage is to consolidate and amplify what is already there. Some suggestions will be given as to how the simpler factual information may be memorised, followed by similar suggestions for dealing with more complex ideas such as those found in *essay plans*, always remembering that revision is a personal matter and that some of these suggestions may not suit everyone.

Techniques for memorising

- **Simplicity and clarity**

A memorable title and clearly defined sub-headings are obviously the easiest to remember.

- **Mnemonics**

These are a great help to some people, but don't waste time trying to invent them unless they are obvious. As an example, Hitler's rise to power might be dealt with under the following headings:

(a) the imperfections of the *Versailles* settlement
(b) the weakness of the *Weimar* government
(c) *Hitler's* beliefs
(d) the *appeal* of Hitler's programme to different classes
(e) *tactics* employed by the Nazis
(f) Hitler's use of his powers as *Chancellor*
(g) the steps by which *Hitler* became a dictator

The mnemonic **VW HATCH** may be obtained from the initial letters of the words which have been put in italics. For those who draw well, this might be represented by a sketch of a hatchback car.

- **Diagrams**

These are particularly memorable for some people; others find it easier to remember words. You should know by now which category you're in. Remember that all diagrams should be simple, clear, without unnecessary detail and, if possible, of a memorable outline.

All reworking of notes is helpful for *recall*, but the change from linear notes to diagrammatic notes will be particularly useful in aiding memory since it involves plenty of thought. Diagrams *compress* information so that it is often possible to put several pages of notes on to one A4-page diagram.

Types of diagram

(a) Time-lines

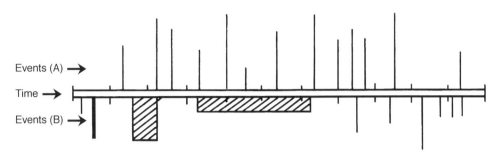

OR

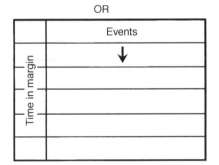

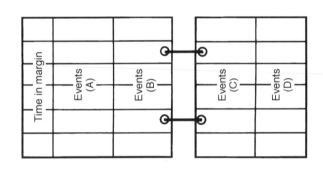

A similar system can also be used for COMPARISONS:

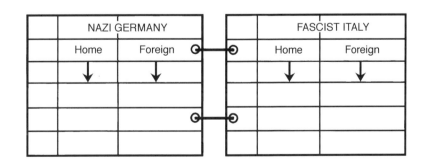

(b) Circular notes (1)

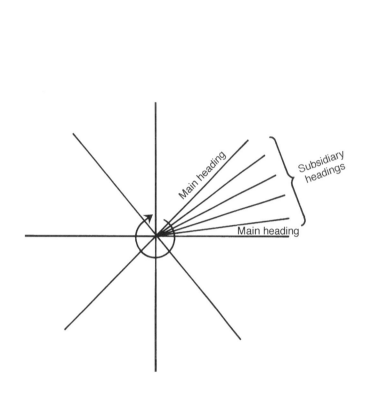

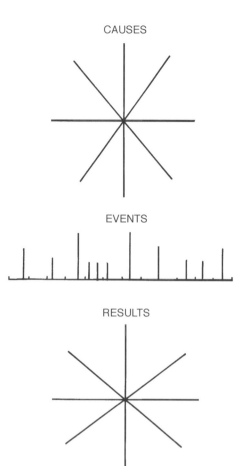

CAUSES

EVENTS

RESULTS

(c) Circular notes (2)

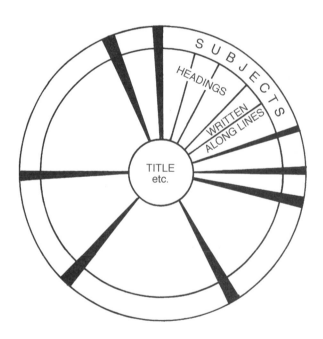

(d) 'Family trees'

These can also be used for organisations:

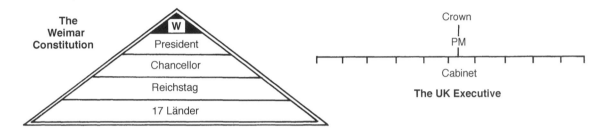

The Weimar Constitution

| W |
| President |
| Chancellor |
| Reichstag |
| 17 Länder |

Crown

PM

Cabinet

The UK Executive

(e) 'Flow diagrams'

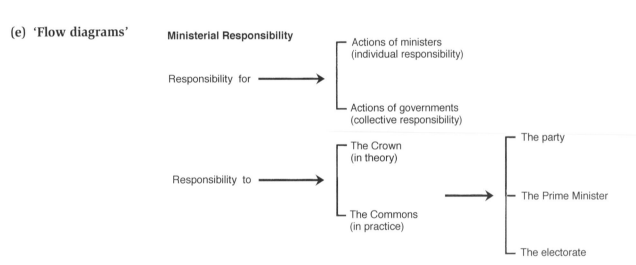

Ministerial Responsibility

Responsibility for ⟶ Actions of ministers (individual responsibility)

Actions of governments (collective responsibility)

Responsibility to ⟶ The Crown (in theory)

The Commons (in practice) ⟶ The party

The Prime Minister

The electorate

These are also useful for industrial processes and scientific experiments.

(f) 'Mind maps'

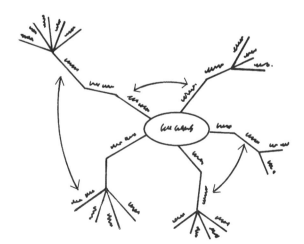

These can be used to show a lot of information on one sheet. *Remember:* Start at the centre and work outwards, *Print* along lines, *Join* important facts. You can use mind maps and linear notes together.

- **Learning by heart**

Some important facts (definitions, some memorable quotations, a few important dates, the spelling of key words) will have to be learnt by heart. The secret of success lies in constant repetition: definitions and quotations can be written out and checked, dates and spellings may be repeated to friends, diagrams should be repeatedly drawn until they are accurate.

- **'Links'**

The linking of any fact with others will always help recall: dates, for instance, will be much easier to remember once they can be linked with other dates – this is where **chronological charts**, particularly those with several vertical columns, are so useful.

The revision of essay plans and complex diagrams

- Make these as portable as possible by reducing their size in a photocopier. Use card rather than paper. Portable revision cards will enable you to memorise them during the many spare moments you'll find during the day: in queues, on buses, etc. Keep cards in plastic wallets to protect them.
- A portable tape-recorder can also play a useful part in revision. Material to be learnt can be dictated onto tape (much more quickly than you can write it) and played back at any time. It would be possible to dictate **all your MEPs for all your chosen topics onto one tape** and this could be played over as often as required. Learning by hearing your own voice repeating information is an alternative to reading and re-reading material – you may find it easier to learn this way! You might be able to swap tapes with friends who are revising in the same way.

Testing: You'll already have been tested by 'mock' exams and 'timed' essays before you sit the actual papers. If you've been criticised for writing answers that are too short or too long, it's up to you to do something about it. **Do not assume that everything will be OK on the day of the exam!**

    If your answers are too long, that's probably the result of poor planning. Check your *MEPs*. Are you using too many paragraphs? Are you including too much detail? Are your introductions and conclusions too long and too 'wafflish'? Above all, are you answering the question that was set and not filling your essay with a lengthy description of events?

    If your answers are too short, make sure that you aren't wasting time during the exam – you should be planning and essay-writing for at least 90% of the time allowed. **Don't** try to make your essays longer by 'waffling', look again at your planning and consider whether you're supplying enough detail in each paragraph – or, indeed, enough paragraphs. Check your introductions and conclusions to make sure they include what is required.

    Finally, remember that your eventual objective is twofold:

(i) to be able to compose an *MEP* for the answer to any suitable question on your various revision topics ('suitable' in the sense that it is not a 'rogue' question which unexpectedly explores some new facet of the subject or 'slants' the question in a novel way);

(ii) to be able to write in full each paragraph in your *MEP*.

    In *(i)*, you'll be depending on correct question analysis, probably with some help from answers to *related questions* in the *specimen essays*.

    In *(ii)*, you'll usually need to adapt paragraphs which come from the *specimen essays*, or which you've composed, in note or diagram form, during your revision.

Thus the writing of paragraphs in an exam essay doesn't come from reproducing any that have been learnt by heart, but rather from a 'triggering' of the knowledge, already in paragraph form,

which you've acquired during your revision and can adapt to the particular requirements of the essay in question.

In this way you will be able to avoid the mistake which examiners often notice, that of answering one question with the material learnt for the answer to another. Thorough question analysis and the avoidance of learning paragraphs by heart should prevent this mistake from occurring.

What about the time during the examination period after you have completed the first paper? You must continue to practise **recall** in all your subjects during this time, so you must work out a new *revision timetable.*

How much revision you do on the day before an exam is a matter of personal preference, but don't use the immanent exam as an excuse to do nothing! Nor must you waste those days on which you have no papers, however tempting it is to relax!

Now you're ready to come to the exam room confident, relaxed (but not too much), fit to work flat out for as long as the paper lasts.
Good luck!

Further Reading

From the vast number of books on this period, I've selected below those from which I've quoted most often in the essays in this book; they're the sources upon which I've relied in my study of the subject and many will be available in good bookshops or school and college libraries.

Communist Russia

The prescribed texts for the Oxford and Cambridge Board's Paper 16 are: M. McCauley (ed.), *Octobrists to Bolsheviks, Imperial Russia 1905–1917* (Arnold, 1984), out of print but available from the Oxford office of the Board at £5.00; M. McCauley (ed.), *The Russian Revolution and the Soviet State 1917–1921* (Macmillan, 1984 reprint). Another useful collection of documents and commentary is John Daborn's *Russia: Revolution and Counter-revolution 1917–1924* (CUP, 1991). For Stalin, there are the usual documentary extracts in Martin McCauley, *Stalin and Stalinism* (Longman, Seminar Studies in History, 1983); F.W. Stacey, *Stalin and the Making of Modern Russia* (Arnold, 1970) is another collection.

The revolutions of 1917 and Lenin's rule are covered in Michael Lynch, *Reaction and Revolutions: Russia 1881–1924* (Hodder and Stoughton, Access to History, 1992) and Anthony Wood, *The Russian Revolution* (Longman, Seminar Studies in History, second edition 1986). Both are essential reading. Edward Acton, *Rethinking the Russian Revolution* and Chris Ward, *Stalin's Russia* (both Edward Arnold, Reading History Series) are quite hard going but important for the results of modern research, both British and Russian. Alec Nove, *An Economic History of the USSR* (Penguin, 1970) is the classic text on economic history; Leonard Schapiro, *The Communist Party of the Soviet Union* (Methuen, second edition 1970) deals with more than the party in the USSR. Two useful general histories are L. Kochan, *The Making of Modern Russia* (Penguin, 1977) and G. Hosking, *A History of the Soviet Union* (Fontana, revised edition 1990). D. Shub, *Lenin* (Penguin,

1966) is a hostile treatment; T. Cliff, *Lenin* (Bookmarks) is more sympathetic. Alan Bullock, *Hitler and Stalin* is easy to read and up-to-date; other biographies are I. Deutscher, *Stalin: A Political Biography* (Penguin, 1977) and Adam P. Ulam, *Stalin: The Man and his Era* (Allen Lane, 1974). Finally, John Reed's *Ten Days that Shook the World* (Penguin, 1966) should not be missed.

Fascist Italy

D. Mack Smith is the best known author, writing in English, on this period. M. Clark, *Modern Italy 1871–1982* (Longman, 1984) is a good up-to-date survey. Mark Robson, *Italy: Liberalism and Fascism 1870–1945* (Hodder and Stoughton, 1992) in the excellent 'Access to History' series, is invaluable, as is Martin Blinkhorn, *Mussolini and Fascist Italy* in the 'Lancaster Pamphlets' series, published by Methuen (1984).

Nazi Germany

The Oxford and Cambridge prescribed texts are A. Hitler, *Mein Kampf*, edited by D.C. Watt (Hutchinson), vol. II, chs 1–3 and 5, and J. Noakes and G. Pridham, *Nazism 1919–1945* (University of Exeter), vols 1, 2 and 3. J.W. Hiden, *The Weimar Republic* (Longman, Seminar Studies, 1974) covers the 1920s and early 1930s; D.G. Williamson, *The Third Reich* (Longman, Seminar Studies, 1982) and Geoff Layton, *Germany: The Third Reich, 1933–45* (Hodder and Stoughton, Access to History series, 1992) are essential introductions to the period; John Traynor, *Europe 1890–1990* (Macmillan, Challenging History series, 1991) covers Mussolini's Italy, Soviet Russia and Nazi Germany in less detail but in a modern format.

Biographies of Hitler include Alan Bullock's *Adolf Hitler: A Study in Tyranny* (Penguin, 1962) and his later *Hitler and Stalin*, which has important comparative insights. General works on the Third Reich include Ian Kershaw, *The Nazi Dictatorship* (Edward Arnold, third edition 1993) and *The Hitler Myth* (OUP, 1989); K.D. Bracher, *The German Dictatorship* (Penguin, 1973); and J.C. Fest, *The Face of the Third Reich* (Penguin, 1979). Social history is covered by R. Grunberger, *A Social History of the Third Reich* (Penguin, 1974) and *Life in the Third Reich*, edited by Richard Bessel, (OUP, 1967). For foreign policy, consult William Carr, *Arms, Autarky and Aggression* (2nd edition, Arnold, 1971), Richard Overy, *The Road to War* (Macmillan, 1989), A.J.P. Taylor, *The Origins of the Second World War* (Hamish Hamilton, 1991) and *The Origins of the Second World War*, edited by E.M. Robertson (Macmillan student edition, 1971). For Nazi anti-Semitism, see Lucy S. Davidowicz, *The War Against the Jews* (Penguin, 1987).

General Works on Twentieth-Century Europe

Stephen J. Lee's *The European Dictatorships, 1918–1945* (Routledge, 1987) is excellent, as is his *Aspects of European History, 1789–1980* (Methuen, 1982). Useful reference books include *Chambers' Biographical Dictionary* and *Chronicle of the Twentieth Century* (Longman). Pamphlets published by the Historical Association (particularly Alec Nove, *Stalinism*, New Appreciations in History, No. 5) are always good value; there are also many important articles in such publications as *History Today*, *Modern History Review* and *History Review*. Nor should audio and visual aids be forgotten; some of the tapes sold by Audio Learning Ltd and Sussex Tapes are particularly useful for Soviet history and Hitler's foreign policy, providing significant information in a discussion format and an excellent use for the ubiquitous 'Walkman'.

essay questions

Communist
Russia

Essay 1

How important was the effect of World War One on the political, economic and military systems of Russia?

Tackling the question

Although many syllabuses on this period begin in 1917, it's obviously necessary to know how World War One affected the tsar's autocratic government in Russia and paved the way for the revolutions to come. Here is a straightforward 'long question' (in the sense that it provides plenty of information to help you plan the answer). Your essay plan will obviously be based on the effects on the political, economic and military systems – the main decision for you to make will be how many paragraphs to allot to each. Here I've decided to give **two** paragraphs to the political system and **one** each to the other two topics. **Remember that the number of paragraphs you give to a topic help to indicate to the reader how important you judge that topic to be in your answer to the question**. Look at my conclusion to see how the summary of these two paragraphs on the political effects strengthens the importance of these effects in the final summary.

Answer

Guidance notes

Historians have long debated the question of whether Russia was heading for revolution in 1914. 'Pessimists' (to use Stephen Lee's term) agree with the Soviet view that 'revolution was inevitable, with or without the assistance of a catalyst like war'. 'Optimists' believe that 'tsarism could have struggled on, at least into the foreseeable future', building on Stolypin's economic reforms and introducing enough basic changes to satisfy the Liberals: 'Give us ten more years and we are safe', observed Shidlovsky before 1914. But many writers have also emphasised the fragile nature of the Russian state, with its growing polarisation between 'the vast bulk of privileged society and the tsarist regime' as well as 'between workers and educated, privileged society' (Haimson). It is, however, possible to observe certain undisputed effects of the war on the political, economic and military systems of Russia, between 1914 and 1917.

Introductions. Here is our first example of how to write an introduction. In this case, I wanted to use the introduction to introduce the reader to the terms 'Optimist' and 'Pessimist' and to define them so that I could refer to them again in the conclusion.

The outbreak of war produced a surge of patriotic emotion and national consolidation. Only the Social Democrats in the Duma repudiated the war and the five Bolshevik members were arrested at the end of 1914; Liberals, on the other hand, welcomed the alliance with Britain and France as a democratising force in Russia. But the tsarist autocracy soon showed that it was unable to cope with the strains of total war. Nicholas II was revealed as an unsuccessful military leader, but his decision to take over supreme command in 1915 may have been most damaging in the reliance now placed on the tsarina and Rasputin to rule the country while he was at headquarters. Their attempt to do so was disastrous, 'corrupt fools succeeded corrupt oafs in the highest positions in the land'; the bureaucracy, already by 1914 'largely sterile and obstructive', had by 1917 become paralysed and unable to face threats from within or without; co-operation with the Duma and other public organisations (the Zemstras, the urban dumas and the War Industry Committees) had been briefly possible in 1915, but the opportunity was missed. Sazonov saw the government as 'hanging in the air [with] no support either from above or below'.

Spelling and technical terms. Are you a bad speller? Then you've got to get down to learning to spell the important words in the syllabus – examiners don't take kindly to candidates who cannot spell the most commonly used words. Similarly, with technical terms: there must be no doubt in the reader's mind whether you understand the meaning of **Progressive bloc, Duma, Kadet, Liberals, 'cadre', Cossack**.

Opposition grew with the increasing paralysis of the autocracy. The Progressive bloc in the Duma became a focal point of political resistance and Miliukov, the Kadet leader, spoke for many in his famous 'Is it stupidity or treason?' speech of November, 1916. But the Liberals were always afraid of revolution, as were many of the middle class they represented. The Petrograd working class, in contrast, was influenced by 'cadre' workers, veterans of prewar campaigns, with clear ideas of what they wanted and the determination to achieve it. Faced with growing opposition and unwilling to co-operate with it in any way, the autocratic state depended on the loyalty and efficiency of the forces of repression, but the police were ill-trained and corrupt, Cossack loyalty had been eroded by 'financial grievances and inadequate land grants', while army officers and men were becoming more hostile to the prospect of 'police' duties.

Use of statistics. No, you haven't got to learn lists of figures by heart. One of the important uses of your revision time is to sort out a short list of exact statistics which you should commit to

Such duties were becoming increasingly necessary as three years of total war proved too great a challenge for the Russian economy. The financial stability gained by 1914 was destroyed as the government printed money to sustain an expenditure of 17,000 million roubles between 1914 and 1917. Rampant inflation followed: average earnings doubled while the price of food quadrupled (1914–16). Severe problems in the production and distribution of foodstuffs were allied to the rise in food prices by 1916. Peasants hoarded grain when inflation made trading unprofitable; towns and cities suffered badly – particularly Petrograd which was far from the main food-producing regions and inundated by refugees. But it was the failure of the transport system which was the greatest cause of Russian suffering. By 1916, the railway system had virtually collapsed. 'Before the war, Moscow had received an average of 2,200 wagons of grain per month; by February 1917 this figure had dropped to below 700 ... [while] the capital received only 300 wagon-loads of grain' (Lynch).

The effects of the war on the army must not be exaggerated. Casualty figures were high, but not that much higher than those of other belligerents. Equipment was lacking (although Russia produced more shells than Germany in 1916); the breakdown of the transport system had added greatly to the army's problems by 1916 (and yet the Brusilov offensive gained considerable success); the tsar's decision to assume direct command of the army in 1915 has been much criticised, but it at least reflected his determination to replace the Grand Duke Nicholas, whose nerves had been shattered by the disasters of the first year of the war and who had allowed himself to become allied with Duma critics of the government. In all, the Russian army was not on the verge of collapse in 1917, its structure was not undermined and its discipline was still intact.

Historians would agree that the war served to destabilise the tsarist regime, to heighten opposition to it from many of its former supporters, to show plainly that the Russian economy could not stand the strain of total war and to make it more doubtful whether the coercive forces available to the tsar (particularly the army) could be trusted to crush unrest at home. As between the views of the 'Optimists' and 'Pessimists' (whether Russia's evolution towards capitalism and a western liberal democratic system was rudely interrupted by a fortuitous war, or whether the war merely hastened a process governed by Marxist inevitability which was bound to end in the overthrow of both capitalism and tsarism), the debate continues.

memory. The last sentence in the paragraph is an important one and the exact words are worth remembering if you're good at learning by heart; if not, put the meaning in your own words, including the two important figures 2,200 and 700.

Conclusions. This begins with a **summary** of the effects of World War One on Russia's political system, the economy and the army. It continues with an admission that the debate between 'Optimists' and 'Pessimists' continues (**never be afraid to admit that it's impossible to give a final answer to a question**). You might say that the effect of World War One on the February Revolution is outside the scope of the question; normally, I would agree, but in this case the connection between the two is so important that the point is worth making **after you've answered the question**.

Mini essay plan

Paragraph 1 Introduction. The views of 'Optimists' and 'Pessimists' concerning the chances of revolution in Russia in 1914.

Paragraph 2 The effect of war on the tsarist political system.

Paragraph 3 The growth of opposition to the tsar.

Paragraph 4 The challenge to the Russian economy presented by the war.

Paragraph 5 The effects of the war on the Russian army.

Paragraph 6 Conclusion. The war affected the political system, the economy and the army. The debate over the chances of revolution after 1914 continues.

General comments

Related questions

1 How important was the First World War in causing the collapse of tsarism in early 1917?

2 How far did Russia's war against Germany and Austria prepare the way for the February Revolution of 1917?

3 'Tsarist government had become chaotically incompetent.' To what extent does this explain the downfall of tsardom in March 1917?

Questions on the effects of World War One on tsarist Russia can normally be answered by using the three topic headings: **political, economic, military**. You'll find that this is often true of other topics and this will help your revision a lot. In this case, you can make a start by considering how far the paragraphs used in the specimen essay might be used to answer the related questions.

Essay 2

> ‘Not an overthrow from without, but a
> collapse from within.’ Consider this verdict
> on the February Revolution of 1917.

Tackling the question

This is the first question containing a **quotation. Don't be frightened by these: they are often easier than other types of question!** Here the quotation provides a straightforward choice: ‘overthrow from without or collapse from within’? Remembering to apply our three rules for quotation questions (see Introduction,

Answer 11(c)), the phrase ‘consider this verdict’ is the same as ‘discuss’ and requires you to agree, disagree or partly agree with the statement in the quotation; your verdict will appear in your conclusion and it may agree with one part of the quotation but not the other.

Answer

Guidance notes

Lenin defined the essentials of revolution as follows: ‘first that a majority of workers ... should fully understand that a revolution is necessary and be ready to sacrifice their lives for it; secondly that the ruling classes be in a state of governmental crisis ... a crisis which weakens the government and makes it possible for the revolutionaries to overthrow it rapidly’. To understand the pressures from within and without which caused tsardom to collapse in the first revolution of 1917, it is necessary to consider the situation at the beginning of that year (the personal weakness of the tsar, the chaos into which his government had fallen, the economic and military crises faced by Russia and the growing opposition to tsarist rule), the events of the revolution itself and the reasons for its success.

Like Charles I of England and Louis XVI of France, Nicholas II was a good husband and father; unfortunately, again like them, he was also devoted to, and dominated by, an unpopular foreign wife, who constantly urged him ‘to be a man’ and saddled him with the disastrous weight of Rasputin's advice. The war placed a new burden of responsibility on the tsar, one which he was more

Introductions. I've used a longish quotation here to begin my answer. It could be shortened by putting it in your own words. Note that the **use of (...)** to cut out unnecessary words can shorten quotations a lot; the final version must read sensibly, however. A well-chosen quotation makes a good start to an essay, but don't waste time in an exam trying to recall one!

Comparisons. Comparisons with historical events or persons in other countries are always valuable and ‘mark-worthy’, but make sure the comparison is apt and relevant.

and more obviously unable to bear. The February rising was not the first move against him; during 1916 there had been a number of attempted palace coups, such as the assassination of Rasputin in December. A ruler who could allow the country to be controlled by a debauched monk could not expect the continued support of the aristocracy.

Punctuation. The most important use of punctuation in an essay is for a **list**, which should be introduced by a colon (:) while the parts of the list are separated by commas (,) or if they are lengthy phrases, particularly containing commas, by semi-colons (;).

Nor was the system of government any help to its beleaguered ruler. Oppressive and inefficient before the war, the short-comings of the bureaucracy were now glaringly apparent: its failure to produce military victory now overshadowed by its failure to halt inflation, maintain the railway system and feed the towns – particularly Petrograd. Chaos at the top – for no effective ministry could work with the tsarina and Rasputin – was allied with refusal to collaborate with the Duma, for the tsarist system was 'structurally … incapable of co-operating with and accommodating the increasingly vigorous role sought by the middle classes' (Acton).

Three years of total war proved equally disastrous for the economy. Russia entered the war with a weak arms industry and relatively poor communications, 'quite unprepared for the huge expenditure of arms and ammunition, particularly artillery, which modern war required' (Nove). Shortages of equipment, particularly shells, led to prolonged retreat in the spring of 1915 and although munitions production improved considerably in 1916, the armaments industry had absorbed most of Russia's engineering capacity, making it impossible to maintain the railway network and supply the towns with food. It is hardly surprising that some historians see economic failures as the basic reason for the 'decline and slide into revolution in 1917'.

How strong was the opposition? In the Duma, the moderate Kadet leadership was inhibited by fear of revolution. But there were signs that some of the bourgeoisie thought differently. The Moscow-based leadership of the War Industry Committees, the rank-and-file employees of the Union of Towns and the Union of Zemstvos, even the Progressive Party in the Duma, all showed a willingness to criticise the government and find common ground with socialist parties. Bolsheviks saw the February Revolution as a 'conscious assault on tsarism, spearheaded by the proletariat'. Modern research has suggested that a substantial part of this 'spearhead' were veterans of previous campaigns, 'cadre' workers who used their pre-war experience to sustain and spread strikes, lead demonstrations and plot the defection of garrisons. But the claims for Bolshevik and proletarian leadership cannot be sustained. As Acton says: 'the motivation of the masses was very much their own: a determination ... to effect a fundamental shift in power away from managers, officers and land-owners towards workers, soldiers and peasants'.

The February Revolution lasted from 18 February to 4 March. A strike at the Putilov steel works was joined by women and other workers on 23 February. Two days later the strike was general, factories were occupied and police and Cossacks were allying themselves with the demonstrators. The tsar ordered General Khabalov to restore order but by 27 February most of the Petrograd garrison had mutinied, the Duma had defied the tsar's order to disband, a Soviet of Workers' and Soldiers' Deputies had been established and 'Dual Power' was born. On 2 March, the tsar abdicated and the following day the Provisional Government took office, supported (with reservations) by the Soviet.

Why did the revolution succeed in bringing down the Romanov dynasty, which had lasted three hundred years, in less than a fortnight? The tsar was absent from Petrograd and deserted by his most committed supporters: high-ranking army officers who first suggested that he should stand down, aristocratic members of the Duma who led the refusal of that body to disband, army and police chiefs who told him they could no longer control the capital. The rest of the country followed Petrograd's lead and Trotsky was right when he emphasised that 'neither at the front nor at the rear was there a brigade or regiment prepared to do battle for Nicholas II'.

Certainly the ruling classes were 'in a state of governmental crisis' and it was the collapse from within – above all the desertion of the coercive forces which had saved the regime in 1905 – which brought an end to Romanov rule, as:

> 'Like the chewed stump of a fag
> We spat the dynasty out.' (Mayakovsky)

Conclusion. A suitable quotation is a good way to finish a conclusion, but make sure that it is really relevant to your answer.

Mini essay plan

Paragraph 1 Introduction. Lenin's 'essentials of revolution'.

Paragraph 2 The personal weakness of the tsar and the disastrous combination of the tsarina and Rasputin.

Paragraph 3 The failures of autocratic government and its inability to co-operate with the middle classes.

Paragraph 4 The effect of total war on the Russian economy.

Paragraph 5 The strength of the opposition.

Paragraph 6 The events of the revolution.

Paragraph 7 Reasons for the success of the revolution.

Paragraph 8 Conclusion. It was collapse from within which brought the end of Romanov rule.

Related questions

1 Why was so little effort made to save tsardom in February 1917?

2 How important is the character and personality of Nicholas II to an understanding of the reasons for the February Revolution?

3 How far do you agree with Trotsky that the February Revolution of 1917 succeeded because of the attitude of the Russian armed forces?

General comments

The **causes** of the February Revolution is an obviously popular question. Such questions are often of the **relative importance** type (see Introduction, Answer 11(b)), where one cause is specified in the question and you are required to compare the importance of that with other chief causes. **Related questions 2 and 3** are examples of this; the specimen essay is a variation where you are asked to compare the truth of two different verdicts on the revolution. Paragraphs 2–7 thus provide you with the basis for an answer whichever of the causes is featured in the question.

Essay 3

'The Provisional Government was doomed
to failure because its authority was nominal
rather than real.' Discuss.

Tackling the question

Another quotation – you see, they're pretty popular! But what other type of question can you find here? You're right, it's the **relative importance** type again. It's pretty obvious that the most likely type of question on the unsuccessful Provisional Government will focus on the reasons for its failure. Wherever questions deal in causes, the relative importance approach is the most likely, although the question may make efforts to conceal this (see general comments below).

Remember also that 'discuss' means do you agree, disagree or partially agree with what the quotation claims.

Answer

Guidance notes

'The Provisional Government, led by Prince Lvov, was the old duma in a new form' (Lynch). Its very name casts doubts on its legitimacy – indicating that it was a temporary government, holding office until the election of the Constituent Assembly – and its leader could claim its origin lay only in the 'unanimous revolutionary enthusiasm of the people'. In addition, it was forced to share power with the Petrograd Soviet, which refused to join the government and held a watching brief over its actions, but was equally ready to restrict those actions, as in its famous 'Soviet Order Number One', which declared that all military orders issued by the government would only be obeyed if they were approved by the Soviet. Thus the Provisional Government came to be judged solely on its effectiveness in dealing with the enormous problems which faced the nation. It is necessary to examine these problems, and the government's response to them, before deciding whether its nominal authority was the chief cause of its failure.

Introductions. Again, I use a **quotation** to begin the answer, but this time it's a much shorter one. This is just the sort of short quotation it's worth learning by heart: it's likely to be an excellent beginning to many essays on the Provisional Government. But if you've done this, remember that this quote will not suit all questions on this topic; whereas it could begin an answer to **related questions 1 and 2**, it wouldn't be so suitable for **3**.

The 'Dual Power' system immediately raised the question of the government's authority. The police had been replaced by 'a thoroughly decentralised and feeble militia system' (Acton); the Cossacks could no longer be relied upon; as the Minister of War pointed out, 'the Soviet of Workers' and Soldiers' Deputies [enjoyed] all the elements of real power, since the troops, the railroads, the post and telegraph are all in its hands'. Thus the Provisional Government could never depend on its army, and was unable to resort to force to impose its orders on workers, peasants, even Bolsheviks.

Nor were these policies, strongly supported by the middle and upper classes, likely to be well received by the urban workers and the peasants. Between February and April, the government and the Soviet worked in reasonable harmony, producing typically liberal reforms: an amnesty for political prisoners, an eight-hour day for factory workers, recognition of trade unions and the granting of full civil and religious freedoms. But when Lenin produced his April Theses – with their enticing slogans of 'Peace, Bread and Land' and 'All Power to the Soviets' – it became clear that the fragile consensus of 'Dual Power' would no longer hold and that the Provisional Government must face its three most serious problems on its own.

Further reading. This threefold division of the views of historians is based on the plan used by **Edward Acton** in *Rethinking the Russian Revolution*, published by Edward Arnold in the Reading History series. This is a tough book in places, but is well worth the effort if you want to explore particular topics.

Historians are agreed that the failure to give land to the peasants was suicidal for the Provisional Government. There is less agreement on why this happened. The traditional liberal view is that this was 'another instance of the government's internal division, legalistic myopia and political ineptitude' (Acton); Soviet historians see the failure simply as inevitable, given the class orientation of the government; modern research has highlighted the deliberate policy of delay followed by the Kadets in their insistence on postponing action until the Constituent Assembly was in place. Whatever the reason, the delay was disastrous. The peasants would have none of it (a typical resolution from Samara province demanded that 'the land must belong to those that work it with their hands, to those whose sweat flows') and they soon dominated many of the Land Committees – ironically set up by the government to examine land claims – and began to use them to direct the seizure of estates.

The Provisional Government similarly failed to solve the major problems of the economy: an accelerating breakdown in trade, the railway system facing final collapse, falling industrial production leading to less incentive for the peasants to market their grain, the ill-conceived plan for a government monopoly of grain purchased at fixed prices, food shortages worsening in the towns, massive deficit spending fuelling already serious inflation – all providing immense economic hardship, especially for the urban working class. In short, 'the government failed to cater for the needs of the workers and payed the political price' (Acton) – including factory committees demanding workers' control and the appearance of armed Red Guards in industrial areas.

Most important of all, why did the Provisional Government fail to give peace to the suffering country? The war certainly exaggerated its problems and made their solution much harder. The army could no longer be used as a coercive instrument by the government and the transfer of land to villagers was impossible since it would result in mass desertion; the war's effect on the budget, the transport system, industrial production and the provision of grain was apparent to all. The failure to remove the cause of so much misery may have sprung from patriotism, the desire to honour treaties with the Allies or the fear of the results of a German victory for Russia. For Soviet historians, the continuation of the war was inherent in the imperialism of a bourgeois government; there was certainly widespread support for the war among the middle and upper classes, whose mixture of motives included the hope that patriotic fervour might smother social conflict, that the threat of the Constituent Assembly and more radical reform might be postponed and even that the politically unreliable Petrograd garrison might be needed at the front. The Allies showed no interest in a general peace, a separate peace with Germany appeared far too dangerous and so the Russian war effort staggered on, although the failure of the June offensive meant that thereafter it was purely defensive.

It is tempting to conclude that the Provisional Government faced an impossible task. Certainly its lack of real authority was a serious handicap and prevented it gaining widespread support once the first weeks of revolutionary euphoria had given place to the cry of 'All Power to the Soviets!' But it was the failure to solve the enormous problems that beset it which provides the clue to its miserable end in the Winter Palace.

Punctuation. Here's another example of the **'colon list'**. You'll see in subsequent essays how often it's useful.

Conclusions. Here the **relative importance** nature of the question is clearly tackled. While admitting that the cause highlighted in the quotation ('lack of real authority') was 'a serious handicap', the more important cause of the failure to implement Lenin's call for 'Peace, Bread and Land' is acknowledged as the real clue to the collapse of the Provisional Government.

Essay 3

Mini essay plan

Paragraph 1	Introduction. Lack of legitimacy compounded by power-sharing with the Soviet. Provisional Government must be judged on its ability to solve problems.
Paragraph 2	'Dual Power' and the absence of reliable coercive power.
Paragraph 3	Policies could not gain support in the face of Bolshevik slogans.
Paragraph 4	Failure to give land to peasants was suicidal.
Paragraph 5	Failure to solve problems of the economy lost support of urban workers.
Paragraph 6	Failure to stop the war added to problems. General or separate peace impossible.
Paragraph 7	Conclusion. Lack of authority a serious handicap, but failure to solve problems the chief reason for demise.

General comments

Related questions

1 Why did it prove impossible to establish liberal democracy in Russia from March to November 1917?

2 'Peace, Bread and Land.' How far does this Bolshevik slogan sum up the problems faced by the Provisional Government between March and November 1917?

3 Why did Kerensky fall?

Here's another **relative importance** question where it's clear that your first priority is to be able to write three good paragraphs on the Provisional Government's failure to provide 'Peace, Bread and Land'. They would form the backbone of any answer to a question on the causes of the failure of the Provisional Government, together with a paragraph on 'nominal rather than real authority'.

Related questions 1 and 2 will not be difficult to plan on this basis; **Question 3** might need more on Kerensky's character and the sequence of events leading to his fall.

But you can see how related questions can often be answered using very similar material to that provided in the specimen essay.

Essay 4

'No Lenin: no October Revolution.' How important was Lenin's leadership for the success of the Bolsheviks?

Tackling the question

Here's a question which concerns one of the great problems that historians try to solve – **the importance of the individual in history**. It is a bit ironic that Marxists should acknowledge the part played by Lenin in the second revolution of 1917, when they argue so often against the power of the individual to alter the flow of the great tides of history. Nevertheless, as the introduction points out, Soviet historians have not been slow to praise Lenin's achievements in the Bolshevik revolution. It is important for you to think about the place of other individuals in your period: Trotsky, Stalin, Mussolini, Hitler, etc. Questions will often focus on their contribution to their period as a whole or at particular turning points in their lives; even within questions not specifically on the part played by individuals you may have to consider their importance.

Answer

Guidance notes

Although Marxists would normally query the role of the individual in history, Soviet historians have always stressed the brilliance of Lenin's leadership in 1917. To criticise this view, it is necessary to investigate why there was a second revolution in 1917, why this was a Bolshevik revolution and what part was played by Lenin, and others, in the success of this revolution.

There can be no doubt that by October, Russia was ripe for revolution. The Provisional Government, lacking legitimacy, bereft of the normal forces of law and order and forced to share power with the Petrograd Soviet, had manifestly failed to solve the three problems which the Bolsheviks summed up in the slogan 'Peace, Bread and Land'. Instead, 'exhausted workers, war-weary soldiers and angry peasants' still faced an uncertain future: 'the working class ... fearful lest it might starve in the

Introduction. The introduction stresses how it is necessary to investigate why there was a revolution in October 1917, why it was a Bolshevik revolution and what part was played by Lenin and others in its success. It's always important to concentrate on the actual question, but the scene must be set if the reader isn't to be assumed to know too much of the background. Also, as is often the case, a concentration on Lenin's leadership to the exclusion of everything else would demand such detailed knowledge that few candidates

Essay 4

would be likely to attempt the question. You'll always have to decide, in planning your answer, how much you can assume that the reader knows.

Further reading. You must be sure of the meaning of the phrase **democratic centralism** if you're going to use it in an essay. This sounds obvious, but it's noticeable how examiners often comment that candidates are ready to include phrases of which they obviously don't know the meaning or are uncertain of the details. Look up democratic centralism (for instance, in the index of **Lynch**) and beware of putting in technical terms because they sound impressive! **The examiner will normally be quick to spot that you don't know what you're talking about!**

Punctuation. The **dash (–)** can be used to sum up what's in front of it. Here, the phrase 'policies that had little appeal to the population' applies to each of the policies 'urged' by Lenin in April. This is a useful punctuation mark – **use it yourself!**

forthcoming winter; the middle class unhappy because the real value of its dividends was falling' (Service). The days of the Provisional Government were clearly numbered; the question remained of what sort of government might replace it.

The fact that the revolution, when it did come, was a Bolshevik revolution appears equally unsurprising. Here Lenin's role seems clear. His greatest achievement was the reshaping of Marxist theory to fit the situation in Russia. According to the theory of 'democratic centralism', the party was to direct the revolution from above and was to be an 'exclusive, tight structured, professional organisation', ruthless in its methods 'because the party is the only historical instrument given to the proletariat to resolve its fundamental tasks' (Trotsky). Similarly, in 1917, again exhibiting essential opportunism, Lenin could claim that, in Russia, the bourgeois and proletarian stages of the revolution could be compressed into one. On his return from Switzerland in April, he was able to persuade the party to accept his April Theses which scorned collaboration with the Provisional Government – thus refusing to prop up the system and letting it collapse in order to build on its ruins – claiming that the Soviet was the only body with the right to govern. He might despise the Soviet, but it could be used, as Lynch indicates, as a base through which the Bolshevik Party could obtain power in the name of the proletariat.

Having gained acceptance for the new strategy at the April Party Congress, Lenin's leadership faltered and he began, as Robert Service shows, to make mistakes which could have been fatal to the party. In April, he was urging the need for a European civil war, the dictatorship of the proletariat and land nationalisation – policies that had little appeal to the population. His ambivalent attitude in the July days – with their massive rioting which gave the Provisional Government the excuse to move against the Bolsheviks – brought the party to the verge of destruction. With its leaders in flight or under arrest, it was only saved from extinction by its part in the defence of the capital against Kornilov's forces. In September, while still in hiding, Lenin was pressing for an immediate seizure of power which would probably have given Kerensky his last chance of suppressing the party while still strong enough to do so. Thus it becomes increasingly hard to see Lenin's faltering leadership as vital for the success of the October Revolution.

Moreover, modern research has cast increasing doubt on the role of the Bolsheviks and their leadership in that revolution. Many writers now see it as a revolution from below, won by the people themselves rather than by any party, as they pressed for action on policies of their own making. What is more, the Bolshevik Party had changed dramatically as its numbers rose from 10,000 in February to 250,000, or more, by October. Now it was a mass workers' party rather than the 'exclusive clique of radical intellectuals' envisaged by Lenin. Its success in October came from its ability to 'articulate the masses' own goals, but it did not create either those goals or the mass radicalism which went with them' (Acton).

Where, then, is Lenin's place in the revolution? Acton claims that 'to stress the party's responsiveness to pressures from below is not to deny the significance of the lead given by Lenin. His prestige within the party was enormous ... his ability to combine theory and practice ... was unique'. The Central Committee was always hard to convince (even the fateful decision in favour of an armed uprising, approved by 10 votes to 2 on 10 October, was so strongly opposed by Zinoviev and Kamenev that they carried their opposition into print and thus, ironically, triggered Kerensky's last attempt to crush the party, so causing the signal for revolt to be given), but it was finally convinced and Lenin's success in achieving this decision, at this moment, was vital for success – 'Trotsky was probably right in stating that no-one else could have put the item [on the agenda] in mid-October' (Service). The Military Revolutionary Committee, headed by Trotsky, planned the actual takeover – and it deserves much more credit than it has been given for this – but however effective the planning, it was the timing of the operation that was important for success.

Robert Service claims that 'there would probably have been a socialist regime in place in Russia by the end of the year whether or not Lenin had existed'. On 10 October, Lenin ensured that it was the Bolsheviks who would attempt to seize power before the end of October, and who would succeed.

Discussion questions. As Answer 11 in the introduction reminds you, you must provide **arguments for and against** the statement in the question. This paragraph and the following one detail Lenin's mistakes after the April Party Congress and describe the **'revolution from below'** which many modern historians see as a better explanation for success. The last two paragraphs attempt to balance the arguments about Lenin's place in the October Revolution.

Mini essay plan

Paragraph 1	Introduction. How brilliant was the leadership of one man, Lenin, in the October Revolution?
Paragraph 2	Why was there a second revolution in 1917? Because of the failure of the Provisional Government to solve its problems.
Paragraph 3	Why was this a Bolshevik revolution? Lenin provides the necessary theorising to justify revolution for Marxists.
Paragraph 4	Lenin's faltering leadership, April–September 1917.
Paragraph 5	The concept of 'revolution from below'.
Paragraph 6	Lenin's contribution rests on his success (10 October) in persuading the Central Committee to support an armed uprising.
Paragraph 7	Conclusion. Lenin had ensured that the Bolsheviks would mount the revolution at a time when it was most likely to succeed.

General comments

Related questions

1 Did the Bolshevik seizure of power in 1917 owe more to their own strengths or to the weakness of their opponents?

2 'A brilliantly organised coup by a handful of extremist conspirators which owed little to any popular support.' Discuss this view of the Bolshevik seizure of power in 1917.

3 Who played the greater part in the success of the Bolshevik revolution of October 1917 – Lenin or Trotsky?

The related questions are something of a mixed bag. In **Question 1**, the answer to the specimen essay question does not offer a lot of help. A lot more evidence on Bolshevik strength and opponents' weakness will be required for a good answer.

Question 2 is interesting in that it sets out a statement of the view that popular support was unimportant in the outcome of the revolution – a view directly opposed to that of the **'revolution from below'**. It's obviously necessary for you to know the details of this theory and the evidence on which it relies. Chapter 8 of *Rethinking the Russian Revolution* is a good place to start.

Question 3 brings in Trotsky's part in affairs – knowledge of another individual is required.

Essay 5

How effective was Soviet foreign policy from October 1917 to the death of Lenin in 1924?

Tackling the question

Questions which examine foreign policy over a period are common. When planning your **revision strategy**, you'll have to decide whether to include foreign policy as one of the topics which you're going to revise.

Revision strategy is the result of your decision on what topics to revise. You should make up your mind about this when you've assembled all your revision material. Rules to follow are:

(i) **Count** the number of topics you've covered during your course.

(ii) **Discover** which are the most popular topics in past papers by analysing the questions.

(iii) **Calculate** the **minimum** number of topics you need to revise by **doubling** the number of questions you have to answer on the paper and adding **two** (e.g. if your paper asks you to answer 4 questions in 3 hours, the minimum number of topics to revise will be $4 \times 2 + 2 = 10$).

(iv) **Choose** the topics on which you have most information (including specimen essays) and those which interest you most.

Answer

Guidance notes

When Trotsky was appointed Commissar for foreign affairs in 1917, he hoped that all he would have to do would be to 'issue a few decrees, then shut up shop and go home'. Foreign affairs, however, was to play a much larger part than Trotsky imagined in the aftermath of the revolution. Its primary aims were the survival of that revolution in a hostile world and support for the world revolution predicted by Marx. Indeed, Trotsky himself was sure that 'if the peoples of Europe do not arise and crush imperialism, we shall be crushed'. In examining the effectiveness of the attempts to combine these often contradictory aims, it is necessary to consider, first, the Treaty of Brest-Litovsk and its terms; then the civil war, the foundation of the Comintern and its early history; and finally, the changes that accompanied the introduction of the NEP.

Introduction. The introduction is a bit longer than usual, but it needs to introduce the two most important (and often contradictory) aims of Bolshevik foreign policy.

The famous Decree on Peace was the first act of foreign policy by the new government, on the day after the revolution. 'Far more Wilsonian than Marxist in language and inspiration' (Carr), it was more effective in its influence on Wilson's Fourteen Points than on Germany or the Allies. Three conflicting views now emerged on the correct approach to ending the war with Germany. Lenin was in favour of an immediate peace, realising that Russia was militarily exhausted and that a German defeat would nullify the harshest peace terms, while German victory would leave the country no worse off. Trotsky counselled delay ('no peace, no war') while awaiting the collapse of the German armies and the outbreak of revolution in Germany. The Left Communists wanted a 'revolutionary war' to be carried on against Germany, 'a partisan war of flying detachments' as Bukharin described it. Trotsky's attempts to prolong negotiations failed; the German forces resumed their now unopposed advance and when Dvinsk fell negotiations had to be resumed with the German terms now more severe. The Central Committee was only persuaded to accept them once Trotsky had changed sides and Lenin had threatened to resign.

Use of statistics. Note how the terms of the treaty are summed up in one sentence. Candidates often put in too much factual detail just because they happen to know it and hope that it will impress the examiner. If it's not necessary, it won't!

The terms were certainly harsh. One third of European Russia (including the food production of the Ukraine) was lost, together with 34% of its population and 32% of its agriculture. No wonder Lenin admitted, 'our impulse tells us to rebel, to refuse to sign this robber peace'. But he added that 'the Russian revolution must sign the peace to obtain a breathing space to recuperate for the struggle'. It was that struggle which gave 'Lenin and Trotsky, as international revolutionaries ... only a limited loyalty to Russia as a nation' (Lynch). World revolution proved illusory, but Lenin's gamble on Germany's eventual defeat paid off.

Use of quotations. If you're going to use quotations well in an essay, you need to be able to fit them into your own sentences without spoiling the grammar. (Let's hope they were grammatical to start with!) In each of the first three sentences of this paragraph, I've used parts of quotations which originally occurred in longer sentences. With a bit of practice, you'll find this quite easy to do.

During the period of the civil war 'foreign affairs in the conventional sense hardly existed' (Condren). The First Congress of the Comintern met at the beginning of March 1919, with Lenin promising 'the victory of communism in the entire world'. But the inaugural meeting was 'a propaganda gesture more than an organisational move' (Schapiro). Lenin's pamphlet, *The Children's Disease of 'Leftism' in Communism*, provided explicit directions for new communist parties in different countries (British communists, for example, should infiltrate the trade unions and support Labour Party leaders 'as the rope supports the hanged man') while later congresses (1920–3) tightened Russian control on the organisation. Brief communist successes in

Hungary, Bavaria, Berlin and other parts of Europe – in particular the Red Army's approach to Warsaw in 1920 – seemed to offer hope of spreading the proletarian revolution, but by 1921 all communist insurrections had been crushed, the Red Army had retreated from Poland and Soviet Russia faced economic devastation.

Lenin's approach to the new situation was as usual realistic. Foreign policy must become defensive and seek allies among the capitalist nations ('Our foreign policy while we are alone and while the capitalist world is strong consists in our exploiting contradictions') while playing on the differences which divided them. Such a 'readjustment' in policy fitted well with the shift from War Communism to the NEP.

An Anglo-Russian trade treaty was signed in March 1921 and a treaty of friendship with Turkey in the same month. In May, a Russo-German trade treaty recognised the Soviet government as the sole government of Russia and promised 'mixed companies' and trading concessions to German industrialists. Economic relations with the United States were established and American machines and industrial equipment began to play their part in Soviet development. In 1922, the Genoa Conference saw the Soviet government accepted as an equal negotiating partner, although no agreement on debts or compensation was reached. More importantly, the agreement at Rapallo saw the end of Russian isolation and the beginning of a special relationship with Germany. The former could now use German technical skills in their factories: the latter had discovered a way of avoiding the military restrictions of the Treaty of Versailles.

When Lenin died in January 1924, the Soviet international position seemed better than at any time since the revolution. The USSR had achieved international acceptance and a reliable relationship with Weimar Germany. She had abandoned her earlier idealistic theories of open diplomacy and disarmament and her 'twin track' approach of attempting to foment revolution in those countries with which she had diplomatic relations had been accepted as normal. The survival of the Bolshevik Revolution was not due to the effectiveness of its foreign policy, nor may the Comintern's attempts to foster world revolution be seen as anything but a failure, but by 1924 the USSR was set on a path which seemed to offer more hope for the future.

Conclusions. The final sentence of the conclusion shows the failures of Bolshevik diplomacy, while the remainder of the paragraph stresses its success. Once again we have a **discussion question** where the answer is to find the balance between success and failure.

Essay 5

Mini essay plan

Paragraph 1	Introduction. The two aims of Soviet foreign policy.
Paragraph 2	Negotiations for the Treaty of Brest-Litovsk.
Paragraph 3	Terms of the treaty.
Paragraph 4	The formation of the Comintern and the absence of world revolution.
Paragraph 5	Lenin's new approach to foreign policy.
Paragraph 6	Trade treaties and agreement with Germany at Rapallo.
Paragraph 7	Conclusion. The aim of survival had been achieved; world revolution had not. But the USSR seemed set on a hopeful path.

General comments

Related questions

1 To what extent had the Soviet Union succeeded in normalising its relations with foreign powers by the end of 1924?

2 What were the principal aims and achievements of Bolshevik foreign policy from October 1917 to October 1920?

3 How do you explain the deep and persistent hostility which Russia encountered in its dealings with the outside world from the end of 1917 to 1924?

What is the most common form of question dealing with foreign policy? It's our old friend 'aims and achievements' (you must have met this phrase before).

Question 2 is an obvious example (but **beware the dates** in the question; it would be only too easy to assume in an exam that the question extended to 1924).

Question 1 can be covered by a lot of what's in the specimen essay (suitably adapted), but would require some extra knowledge of the relations of individual countries with the Soviet Union for a good answer.

Question 3 also requires further knowledge of the nature of the reaction of other countries to the establishment of the Soviet Union.

But the first thing to concentrate on is **aims and achievements**.

Essay 6

Why did the Bolsheviks win the civil war which broke out in the summer of 1918?

Tackling the question

Questions on wars are usually straight-forward and **suitable as revision topics**. They almost always involve the **three Cs: Causes, Course and Consequences**. They are often **explanation questions** (as here, introduced by 'why?'). Here we have a typical question on the course of the war, involving the reasons why one side won.

This is also a **short** question, which gives you no clue as to how to plan your answer. Where you get no help from the question, the trick is to ask yourself for up to **six simple answers** to the question and then to write a paragraph on each. These would include both the reasons why the Bolsheviks won and those which caused their opponents to lose. If you look at the final paragraph of this essay, you can find at least six answers to the question which could have been used as the plan for an answer. In fact, the plan used is a little more complex than that and includes a long paragraph (2) which you may think superfluous. **Always remember that there is no one right answer to a question and it's essential to approach any specimen essay in a critical frame of mind**.

Answer

Guidance notes

Civil wars are frequently nasty, brutish and long. The Russian civil war was no exception and the eventual Bolshevik victory was achieved at enormous cost. To discover the reasons for that victory, one must examine the resistance to the Bolshevik leadership which appeared immediately after the October Revolution, then identify the characteristics of the ensuing civil war, together with its four critical moments, while finally considering the reasons for foreign interventions and their failure.

Introductions. Some writers delight in adapting famous quotations to their own purposes by altering a word or two. The first line of this introduction is an example; can you identify the quotation and say what's been changed?

The immediate military threat to the Bolshevik revolution was ended by the defeat of Kerensky's meagre forces at the Pulkovo Heights at the end of October. Until the beginning of the civil war in the summer of 1918, the main danger to the new government

Technical terms. Do you know the meaning of Sovnarkom? Can you spell it? Most textbooks contain a glossary of Russian terms – **use it!**

came from the parties of the left in Petrograd. Lenin was determined that the Bolsheviks would not share power with other parties of the left: the Mensheviks were weakened by their split into two factions while more immediate danger came from the Social Revolutionaries (SRs) and the railwaymen's union. The dispute over the sharing of power affected the Central Committee and five members resigned in November over the suppression of bourgeois newspapers. The SRs were strongly represented in the Congress of Peasants' Deputies, which met on 11 November. But the SRs were also split – the Left SRs had sided with the Bolsheviks in October – and three of their number became commissars in Sovnarkom, while peasant deputies were added to the central executive committee, together with representatives of the trade unions. The leaders of the railwaymen's union declared themselves satisfied and the revolt within the Bolshevik Party collapsed as the dissidents returned under threat of expulsion from the party. Finally, the Constituent Assembly, where the Right SRs had a clear majority, was dissolved after meeting for a day. A non-violent protest march in Petrograd was the only protest. There were further policy disagreements within the party over the abandonment of collectivisation, the subordination of workers' control by inefficient factory committees to the need for efficient state capitalism and, most dangerously, the Treaty of Brest-Litovsk, which was accepted by a narrow majority in the Central Committee only after Lenin had threatened to resign. Even more important for the immediate future was the growth in the use of terror as a weapon: the Cheka was established by a secret decree in December 1917 and was used extensively against both SR factions in the summer of 1918.

Having seen off the challenge from the left, both inside and outside the party, Lenin's government was now faced with a much more serious challenge from the right. The civil war was a class war, as Lenin claimed, but it was also a war of independence, fought by national minorities, and even, in some places, a struggle for food supplies. Unlike the Great War, it was a war of movement, dictated by the Russian railway system. Cavalry came into its own again and Trotsky's train appeared at critical moments to emphasise the importance of interior lines for the Bolsheviks. Trotsky headed the Supreme Military Council as Commissar for War and created the Red Army by abandoning the slogans of the revolution. Most of the Red Guard and militia units were disbanded, conscription was introduced, 'political commissars' replaced 'soldiers' committees' and ex-tsarist officers were widely used.

Four moments of crisis for the Bolsheviks stand out in the complex manoeuvres of the civil war. The first was the capture of Kazan (August 1918), when a combined Czech and White army threatened to advance on Moscow. In the autumn of 1919, Denikin's capture of Orel again threatened Moscow, while another White army, under Yudenich, reached the suburbs of Petrograd. Finally, the Poles took Kiev in May 1920, but were forced to retreat deep into Poland, then counter-attacked and drove the Red Army to the frontier, where an armistice was quickly signed which eventually became permanent in the Treaty of Riga.

Factual evidence. The course of a complicated war may be simplified by describing a number of critical moments, as has been done here. **Never get bogged down in describing events, unless they are important for your argument; you won't get marks for them!**

Foreign intervention (by Britain, France, Italy, the USA and Japan) complicated the war and provided much needed supplies for the various White armies. At first the intention was to keep Russia in the war; after October 1917, to safeguard Allied war supplies. But there was also much anti-Bolshevik feeling – particularly from Churchill in England and Foch in France – over the separate peace with Germany, the cancellation of foreign debts and the nationalisation of foreign companies, the murder of the tsar and his family and the threat of international revolution. But intervening nations had varied aims, President Wilson would give no support for an anti-Bolshevik war and the armies of Britain and France were too war-weary to fight again in Russia. Indeed, little fighting was done and all western troops were withdrawn by the end of 1920, leaving the Bolsheviks to hail Lenin as the 'Saviour of the Nation' from the invasion of the imperialists.

The reasons for Bolshevik victory are clear. Their geographically central position gave them the advantage of interior lines, control over the main industrial areas of Russia and a favourable position astride the railway system. The people were ruthlessly mobilised for total war; political unity at home, already established by force, was maintained by greater force, while War Communism provided some solution to the appalling problems of supply. The Red Army (with Trotsky displaying his usual genius for ruthless organisation) became an effective fighting force, while Lenin provided equally ruthless leadership and control at the centre. White strategy was largely uncoordinated, with constant supply problems, ineffectual leadership and little military help from the Allies. Both sides resorted to terrorising the civilian populations in the vast war zones; in the end, the Whites failed to win crucial support from the peasants because they were perceived as being on the side of the landlords.

Essay 6

Paragraph 1	Introduction. Civil wars are nasty, brutish and long.
Paragraph 2	Internal threats to the Bolsheviks before the civil war.
Paragraph 3	Characteristics of the civil war. Trotsky and the Red Army.
Paragraph 4	Four moments of crisis for the Bolsheviks.
Paragraph 5	Reasons for foreign intervention and for its failure.
Paragraph 6	Conclusion. Reasons for Bolshevik victory.

Related questions

1 Account for the failure of the Whites in the civil war.

2 How important was allied intervention to the outcome of the civil war?

3 Why did the Red Army win the civil war in Russia from 1919?

General comments

The related questions cover all the likely questions on the civil war. **Question 1** needs some detailed evidence specifically on the failure of the Whites, but a lot of what's in the specimen essay can be used.

Question 2, a **relative importance** question, gives you scope to compare the effect of allied intervention with other reasons for the outcome of the war.

Question 3 needs some detail on the part played by the Red Army in the war, but the other causes of Bolshevik victory will have to be discussed.

In all, this is a good topic to decide to revise in your **revision strategy**: the questions are usually straightforward and the amount of evidence required to answer them is limited. Here is one example of how useful **specimen essays** can be in helping to provide such evidence.

Essay 7

What were the achievements of War Communism and why was it replaced by the New Economic Policy from 1921?

Tackling the question

Here is the first **double question** for you to deal with. The **two essentials** in answering this type of question are **(i)** deciding what balance to give to the two parts of the question in your answer (using six paragraphs as your maximum, this normally comes down to choosing between a 3:3 or 4:2 split); **(ii)** deciding whether to put your **conclusion** to the first part of the question at the end of the section dealing with that part, or to provide a conclusion for both parts in the last paragraph. Here, you'll see that I've used paragraph 4 to give my conclusion on the positive and negative achievements of War Communism, while summing up the reasons for its replacement by the NEP in the last paragraph. The **balance** here is 3:1 between introduction and conclusion; do you think there should have been more on the second question?

Answer

Guidance notes

If War Communism had been the means by which the Bolsheviks won the civil war, the New Economic Policy was the means by which Lenin hoped to win the peace. To measure the achievements of the former, one must examine, firstly, the economic policies pursued between the October Revolution and the outbreak of the civil war in the summer of 1918; secondly, the details of the economic system, called War Communism, which the civil war produced; thirdly, the economic, social and political results of the war and of that policy. An analysis of the situation before the Tenth Party Congress will then indicate the reasons for the introduction of the NEP.

'It was impossible to tell in advance whether we were to stay in power or be overthrown', as Trotsky later wrote about the first months after the revolution. Moreover, Marxist theory provided no model of what the state was to be like after the revolution.

Technical terms. In this essay they come thick and fast and you'll need to have a full understanding of their meaning. Remember that you'll always be faced with the decision as to exactly how much explanation to give of these terms, and how much to assume that the reader knows. It's generally true that candidates tend to write too much explanation; provided that your use of the term makes sense, you can afford to avoid explaining it.

Essay 7

The most important economic problems to be solved were those of the peasants, with their burning desire for land, and those of the industrial proletariat who wanted to rule their working lives through factory committees. In theory, the Bolsheviks stood for collectivisation; in practice, Lenin's Land Decree (26 October) had accepted the need for a tactical compromise by following the SR programme of dividing the estates into countless small plots. In industry, the situation was different. Factory committees soon proved their incompetence and single managers and technical specialists had to replace them. On 2 December, the Supreme Council of National Economy (Vesenkha) was established and state capitalism was born. Initially weak, the new council nevertheless presided over important developments: the banks and railways were nationalised, foreign debts were cancelled, foreign firms were taken over. In 1920, a special State Commission (GOELRO) was created to introduce the nationwide generation of electricity – with Lenin claiming that 'Communism equals Soviet power, plus electrification'.

But this was a dream for the future; the harsh reality of the present and the desperate crisis of the civil war forced Lenin to embark on a vast extension of state control over all aspects of the economy, which became known as War Communism. 'All forms of trade and distribution became a state monopoly ... in industry, large and medium sized concerns were brought under the Glavki, the subordinate bodies of Vesenkha, while smaller ones were supervised by provincial economic councils ... all this was accompanied by an immense mushrooming of bureaucracy' (Wood). Food supply was the responsibility of the Commissariat of Supplies (Narkomprod), at first using committees of poor peasants to extract grain from the kulaks, later turning to coercion and the use of the Cheka and the Red Army in ruthless requisition detachments. Professor Nove sums it up as 'a siege economy with a communist ideology'. It depended on the use of terror as an instrument of political control: 'coercion is necessary', said Lenin, 'for the transition from capitalism to socialism'.

Quotations. This long quotation from **Wood** would not have been learnt by heart. Only the phrase 'an immense mushrooming of bureaucracy' is worth committing to memory.

Punctuation. Note the use of semi-colons to separate the achievements of War Communism.

What were the effects of War Communism, its successes and failures? The crisis of 1921 and the hasty switch to the NEP have tended to obscure these. The civil war was won; a food supply of about one third of the pre-war level was somehow maintained in the towns; the government was able to feed an army of five million. But by 1921, a crisis could no longer be postponed. The

output of large-scale industry had fallen to 14% of 1913 levels, with a workforce reduced to little over a million; one in five of the population was starving and the USA was providing some aid through the American Relief Association. Opposition was growing within the party, both from 'Democratic Centralists', urging the restoration of genuine democracy and debate, and from the 'Workers' Opposition', claiming that industry should be run by the trade unions rather than by managers installed by Vesenkha. Communist Party rule was threatened by virtual guerrilla war between peasants and food detachments in the countryside and by a growing number of strikes in industry. The worst blow was the Kronstadt revolt, six days before the start of the Tenth Party Congress, with the sailors, hitherto the staunchest supporters of the Bolsheviks, urging reforms inspired by striking workers in Petrograd. It was a 'revolt of the proletariat against the dictatorship of the proletariat'.

Lenin, ever the pragmatist, saw that a change of policy was essential. 'Henceforth, peasants would be required to pay a tax in kind (that is, in grain) enabling them to sell their remaining surplus on the open market' (Gatrell). The NEP was born with profound implications for the future: the creation of the new class of 'Nepmen', the necessity for a balanced budget, the end of state subsidies for industry causing massive redundancies and 16% unemployment, later the 'scissors crisis' and the consequent reduction in industrial prices (1924) which marked another victory for the peasants. But Lenin emphasised that the party still had control of the 'commanding heights of the economy' and the resolutions on 'Party Unity' and 'Workers' Opposition' provided 'a highly effective means of stifling criticism of the NEP' (Lynch).

There can be no doubt that the introduction of the NEP was regarded by Lenin as a retreat, if only a temporary one. He had clung to War Communism as long as he could, but the languishing economy and the growing famine forced him to consider alternatives. Peasant risings, strikes in Moscow and Petrograd, and the final explosion of opposition at Kronstadt all convinced him that change was inevitable. Events, rather than any Marxist theory, had provided the stimulus for that change.

Conclusions. Although this conclusion deals with the answer to the second part of the question, reference is made to the answer to the first part in the second and third sentences. This links the two halves of the question together.

Mini essay plan

Paragraph 1 Introduction. War Communism the means for winning the civil war; the NEP the means for winning the peace.

Paragraph 2 The introduction of state capitalism after the revolution.

Paragraph 3 A vast extension of state control in the civil war, known as War Communism.

Paragraph 4 The successes and failures of War Communism, leading to Kronstadt.

Paragraph 5 Aspects of the NEP.

Paragraph 6 Conclusion. The NEP regarded as a retreat by Lenin, but a temporary one forced on him by events.

Related questions

1 'We are now retreating.' (Lenin to party members, describing the NEP, 1921) Why did he feel obliged to introduce the NEP?

2 Do you agree that in the years 1921–4 the economic policy of Lenin's government abandoned Bolshevik principles?

3 How justified would Lenin have been, by the time of his death, in feeling proud of the achievements of his New Economic Policy?

General comments

Looking at the related questions, we can see that the two topics of War Communism and the NEP appear to offer a good choice for our **revision strategy**. **Question 1** is really the same question as that for the specimen essay, in different words. In answering **Question 2**, we can use much of the evidence in the specimen essay, plus a little more on 'Bolshevik principles'. **Question 3** stresses the need to be able to describe the achievements of the NEP, as well as those of War Communism.

If we've enough information about the reasons for the two systems, what they entailed and how much they achieved, we'll probably be able to answer the likely questions on these topics.

Essay 8

'No machinery of repression will be required'
(Lenin's *State and Revolution*, September
1917). To what extent did the development of
the communist state during his lifetime
conform to Lenin's aims and expectations?

Tackling the question

Here we have a **'long'** question which looks complicated. Once you have analysed the question, it can be helpful to re-phrase it as simply as possible in your own words, putting a phrase such as **'the question asks'** in front of it. Here the question would then read something like this: **'the question asks how far Lenin's communist state developed according to his aims and expectations'**. It then becomes clearer that your answer will need a description of Lenin's aims and expectations (what is the difference between them?) and a comparison with the actual development of Bolshevik Russia.

Answer

Guidance notes

The October Revolution was a popular revolution. Workers, soldiers and peasants looked for political leaders who would listen to their demands; they found them in the Bolshevik Party when that party had accepted Lenin's call for 'Peace, Bread and Land'. Once in power, the Bolsheviks pursued policies which had universal approval: they ended the war, legitimised peasant land seizures, backed workers against management and recognised the rights of minority nations to self-determination. At first, it seemed that Lenin's optimistic dismissal of the need for repression might be the pattern for the future. But, as Acton points out, this 'essentially popular revolution ... rapidly gave rise to rigid, centralised, doctrinaire, one-party dictatorship', buttressed by a deliberate policy of terror carried out by a ruthless political police and the Red Army. In discovering how and why the popular revolution was betrayed, we may also come to understand whether Lenin's aims and expectations were also betrayed.

Essay 8

Additional evidence and further reading. Richard Pipes' *Russia Under the Bolshevik Regime* provides, in its last chapter, a thought-provoking summary of conclusions on the revolution and the subsequent Bolshevik government under Lenin. He would certainly add to the reasons why the popular revolution of October 1917 betrayed the claim that Lenin and the Bolsheviks were merely returning to the traditions of tsarist rule (which he calls 'tsarist patrimonialism'). He sees tsarist rule resting on 'four pillars': autocracy, the autocrat's ownership of the country's resources, the autocrat's right to demand unlimited services from his subjects, and state control of information.

If you were to write an essay based on Pipes' theory, he provides you with four paragraph headings; any writer who does this is extremely useful for revision.

The desperate defence of the revolution in the civil war, the authoritarian strains in Bolshevik theory and the natural corruption of power all help to explain the betrayal of the popular revolution. But, as Acton stresses, they do not explain why the people did not succeed in defending their revolution. The civil war seemed to most Russians to pose a choice: 'either to permit the restoration of landlords and the old factory order, to forfeit the gains of 1917, or to rally to the Bolshevik side'. Moreover, the unlikely alliance between peasants and workers which had brought an easy victory in October, was breaking down. Industrial production collapsed, the workforce was halved as workers fled the towns to gain their share of the land, and its morale was undermined by the desperate struggle for food. Those who remained in the towns came to hate the peasants, whose selfishness, they believed, was adding to their misery; they were soon ready to support requisitioning by force. In the villages, conflict centred on the 'Stolypin peasants' whose land was redistributed, returning soldiers and workers who reacted against the authority of the village elders, and the growing antagonism between regions without grain and those that had a little – the former being increasingly ready to appeal to a superior authority which could requisition and ration by force. In these conditions, democracy was always likely to be the loser and the forcible closure of the Constituent Assembly brought little protest.

The machinery of repression available to the state was steadily growing. Lenin had always accepted that it would be used against the bourgeoisie ('Coercion is necessary for the transition from capitalism to socialism ... there is absolutely no contradiction between Soviet democracy and the exercise of dictatorial powers') and the Cheka was created as early as December 1917. Its leader, Dzerzhinsky, told his men that when the revolution was in danger there was no need for justice; Lenin claimed, early in 1918, 'until we apply terror – shooting on the spot – to speculators, we shall achieve nothing'. At the fifth Congress of Soviets (July 1918) the Left Socialist Revolutionaries made their bid to wreck the peace with Germany when two of their members assassinated the German ambassador. In August, Uritsky was killed in Petrograd and Lenin seriously wounded in an assassination attempt. On 5 September, the Red Terror was officially proclaimed. All pretense of legality was abandoned; persecution was directed against whole classes and the chairman of the Eastern Front Cheka told his officers, in November 1918: 'Your first duty is to ask him [the accused] to which class he belongs, what are his origins, his education, his occupation.' The answers to such questions would decide the prisoner's fate. Some within the party protested at this abandonment of 'socialist legality'; most agreed with Lenin: 'This is an arch-war situation. We must work up energy and mass-like terror against counter revolutionaries.' The Red Army was employed with similar brutality against the civilian population in the war zone. Robert Conquest claims that 200,000 died at the hands of the Cheka between 1917 and 1923, with a 'further 300,000 ... as a result of other repressive measures, such as the suppression of peasant risings, strikes and mutinies' (Hosking).

Use of statistics. You'll find further statistical evidence of the effects of Bolshevik rule in the chapter of **Pipes'** book referred to above.

While the civil war continued, the majority grudgingly accepted the need for dictatorship and repression; once it ended, 'popular resentment exploded in strikes, massive peasant unrest, and the famous mutiny at the Kronstadt naval base outside Petrograd' (Acton). The result was the announcement of the first stage of the NEP with the abandonment of requisitioning, but the resolutions on Party Unity and Workers' Opposition, together with the brutal repression of the Kronstadt mutineers, showed that with the Tenth Congress the party had finally sanctified the substitution of itself for the working class. Lenin later admitted, in a letter to Kamenev: 'It is a great mistake to think that the NEP put an end to terror; we shall again have recourse to terror and to economic terror.'

Conclusions. Note how the conclusion covers both **aims** and **expectations**.

Thus died the last hope of a return to the ideals of the popular revolution. Peasants and workers were now too weak and divided to regain control of a party in which the leadership could silence opposition by the efficient use of terror. Lenin's chief aim was always worldwide revolution; his methods were always likely to lead to dictatorship and repression. His expectations are more difficult to fathom, for the Bolsheviks, intent on planning revolution, had given little thought to the sort of state that they intended to set up. There is evidence that Lenin realised the dangers of a 'revolution out of control' during the last two years of his life, but there is little sign that he expected any loosening of the constraints exercised by the machinery of repression, least of all its removal.

Essay 8

Mini essay plan

Paragraph 1

Introduction. The popular revolution of 1917 gives way to dictatorship buttressed by terror. In discovering why this happened, we may discover whether Lenin's aims and expectations were also betrayed.

Paragraph 2

Reasons why the people could not defend their revolution.

Paragraph 3

Development of the machinery of repression.

Paragraph 4

The change to the NEP brought no end to the terror.

Paragraph 5

Conclusion. 1921 saw the disappearance of the last hope of a return to the ideals of the popular revolution. Lenin may have realised that the revolution was out of control, but there is no sign that he wished to lessen or dispense with repression, which he always believed would be necessary for successful socialist revolution.

General comments

Related questions

1 At what point, and in what sense, did Lenin's government become a dictatorship?

2 Examine the political and economic legacy which Lenin in 1924 left to his successors.

3 To what extent did Lenin fulfil his promises to the Russian people of 'Peace, Land and Bread' during the years 1918–24?

A big difference here when we look at these related questions. **Question 1** will require careful consideration in planning an answer; quite a lot of the specimen essay can be used, but the paragraphs will change. **Question 2** will require some additional evidence and another rejig of paragraphs. **Question 3** needs a new approach based on 'Peace, Bread and Land'.

Altogether, it seems that, from the sort of questions asked, Lenin's government is not a particularly suitable topic for a **revision strategy**. It does, however, form an important aspect of another question which continues to fascinate historians, the possible links between Leninism and Stalinism. We will take another look at this in considering **Essay 11**.

Essay 9

Why was it Stalin, rather than Trotsky or Bukharin, who eventually emerged as undisputed leader of the Soviet Union?

Tackling the question

Why Stalin? Historians have written at great length to try to answer this question (**Chris Ward**, *Stalin's Russia*, has a whole chapter on this subject – worth reading if you have the opportunity). Few have admitted what the conclusion to this essay stresses, that there is no single answer to the question. Don't be afraid to use this idea in the future: there are certain questions where it's undoubtedly the right answer. Historians are sometimes too keen to find one explanation of events – preferably one which nobody else has considered!

Answer

Guidance notes

'Stalin's victory over his rivals was neither inevitable nor planned in detail in advance' (Bullock). To understand why the victory occurred, it is necessary first to examine the situation at Lenin's death; then to criticise the traditional view of the events leading to Stalin's triumph, with more detailed comment on the mistakes made by both 'Left' and 'Right'; finally, to analyse the means by which Stalin himself ensured success in his bid for leadership. Then it will be possible to answer the question: Why Stalin?

Punctuation. In this introduction there are examples of the use of the **semi-colon** to divide sentences (remember that you can always divide them with full stops if you feel uncertain of using semi-colons) and of the **colon** to introduce a question.

On 25 May 1922, Lenin had his first stroke. During the next year, 'the leadership of the country was in a peculiar state of provisional impermanence' (Conquest). Until his final incapacitating stroke in March 1923, Lenin was able periodically to take some part in government and Stalin almost wrecked his chances with quarrels over the dismissal of the Georgian national representatives and rudeness to Lenin's wife. During this period, Trotsky seemed the most likely to inherit Lenin's position; Zinoviev and Kamenev, with Stalin very much the junior partner,

formed an uneasy alliance to prevent this happening. As long as Lenin lived and was able to give his backing to Trotsky, the latter was in a strong position; even after Lenin's death, his Testament provided a ticking time bomb to threaten Stalin's future.

Paragraph planning. In this particular topic, the first essential is to provide a clear explanation of the successive phases of Stalin's rise to power. You must have worked this out and be fully familiar with it before you can start to write a good answer to this particular question. Nor must you take up too much precious time and space in describing it to the reader. The second sentence of this paragraph tries to do both these things; can you improve its clarity or shorten its length?

The traditional view of Stalin's rise envisages four phases. In the first, from 1923 to 1925, the troika of Zinoviev, Kamenev and Stalin opposes Trotsky; then, when the first two turn against the NEP and support industrialisation (1925–6), Stalin joins Bukharin in opposing them; in the following year, even though joined by Trotsky in the United Opposition, they are defeated by Stalin, Bukharin and the forces of the right; finally, in 1928–9, Stalin turns against his former allies, Bukharin, Rykov and Tomsky, adopts the policies of the defeated left and emerges as sole leader of the Soviet Union. This traditional view has been subject to considerable criticism. Many historians see it as over-emphasising the divisions in the Bolshevik leadership in the 1920s: differences between right and left were more over detail – particularly the speed of industrialisation and the moment when the NEP might be abandoned – rather than over fundamental principles. Carr and Nove see the economic failure of the NEP as evident by 1928–9; for them Stalin's resort to rapid collectivisation was economically motivated. For Schapiro, on the other hand, the decision was chiefly political: concern over the growing power of the peasantry – in particular the kulak, whom Trotsky saw 'knocking at the door of politics' – was widespread among the party leadership. In addition, Schapiro claims that Stalin saw the controversy over industrialisation as a means by which he might rise to power. It seems clear that Stalin's eventual adoption of the policies of the left was taken more on political than economic grounds.

Sources. In this question, dealing with a topic which has been so widely debated by historians, it's necessary to give the views of leading writers on the subject. Using short quotations is an obvious way of doing this. Don't think that the examiner will believe that you have read the original work, but you'll at least have shown some knowledge of what the author has written.

Bullock finds it hard to explain 'why Trotsky should have misjudged the situation so badly, how far he was affected by illness, why he should have proved so inept in tactics and timing (including being absent on critical occasions), why he should have failed, to the despair of his followers, to rally the support which he could still have won in the party'. Certainly, he underestimated the danger from Stalin – that 'grey blur' as he described him. Filled with self-confidence, highly intellectual, with 'a kind of inability or unwillingness to be at all amiable or attentive to people' (Lunacharskii), he refused 'either to organise his friends or divide his enemies' (Carr). Lynch believes that Stalin won because Trotsky 'lacked a power base ... [his]

superiority as a speaker and writer ... counted for little when set against Stalin's control of the party machine'.

The attack on Bukharin and the right was triggered by the ending of the NEP and the beginning of swift industrialisation and forced collectivisation. Politically, they were weaker than the left, their economic arguments appearing timid and inadequate in a period when the country seemed in danger. A majority of the party were ready to adopt a hard line against the peasants now that the NEP seemed to be failing. Nor was it possible for the right to 'impress their views upon the party while Stalin remained master of the party's organisation ... [he could easily] ... portray the Right as an irresponsible and dangerous clique' (Lynch). Like Trotsky, the Right lacked a power base, apart from Tomsky's chairmanship of the trade unions and Uglanov's leadership of the CPSU's Moscow branch – Stalin used Kaganovich and Molotov to purge both. By early 1929, Bukharin, Rykov and Tomsky were out of office and only retained their party membership after publicly admitting their errors. Bukharin had shown himself no match for Stalin, partly – as his biographer argues – because he was blinded by his passionate belief in the NEP.

How far were Stalin's own actions responsible for his success, rather than the mistakes and weakness of his opponents? Stalin was a passionate, skilful and lucky politician, with an excellent grasp of tactics and a ruthless disregard for loyalty to former allies. More a practical politician than an opportunist – for all the leading Bolsheviks changed their minds on key issues – his great administrative capacity (one nickname was 'comrade card-index') made him the indispensable link in the chain joining party to government and provided him with powers of patronage by which he could place his supporters in key positions so that even if he lost the argument in the Central Committee, he would still win the vote.

No single factor explains Stalin's rise: neither the errors of his opponents nor his own talents and desire for power. Russian history, the 'politics of permanent emergency' (Ward) and Stalin's administrative and political abilities ensured the defeat of his rivals.

Essay 9

Mini essay plan

Paragraph 1	Introduction. Stalin's victory neither inevitable nor planned in advance.
Paragraph 2	The situation at Lenin's death.
Paragraph 3	The traditional view of Stalin's rise and criticism of it.
Paragraph 4	The mistakes and weakness of the left.
Paragraph 5	The mistakes and weakness of the right.
Paragraph 6	Stalin's own actions responsible for success?
Paragraph 7	Conclusion. No single factor explains Stalin's rise. It was due to a combination of Russian history, the 'politics of permanent emergency' and Stalin's own abilities.

Related questions

1 Discuss the view that 'Stalin already held the reins of power at the time of Lenin's death in 1924'.

2 'Stalin's victory over his rivals was neither inevitable nor planned in detail in advance' (Bullock). Do you agree?

3 Do you regard Stalin's rise to power as due more to the mistakes of his rivals than to his own abilities?

General comments

You'll not be surprised to hear that the power struggles of the 1920s are a favourite topic with examiners. Nor is this a bad topic to add to your list during the consideration of your **revision strategy**.

Questions fall into three main categories: **(i)** Stalin's defeat of Trotsky and the left; **(ii)** his later defeat of Bukharin and the right; **(iii)** various aspects of this victory.

The specimen essay combines **(i) and (ii)**; you must be ready for questions which concentrate solely on one or the other. **Questions 1–3** are all of the third category: **Question 1** concentrates on the importance of the offices which Stalin held; **Question 2** queries the inevitability and planned nature of his rise (remember that quotations used in questions can be useful for your own essays); **Question 3** focuses on the mistakes of his rivals (and is a type of **relative importance** question).

Provided that you're quite clear about the sequence of events in Stalin's rise, you don't require much more in the way of evidence than that given in the specimen essay if you're going to be prepared to answer all the likely questions on this topic.

Essay 10

With what justification may Stalin's policies of collectivisation and industrialisation be described as a 'second revolution' in the Soviet Union?

Tackling the question

Another major theme in the Stalinist era. Again, collectivisation and industrialisation have been combined in one question; it's more likely that a question would concentrate on one or the other. It's obvious that you must be aware of the meaning of both 'collectivisation' and 'industrialisation' but it's also necessary to consider carefully the meaning of **'second revolution'**.

Does the scale of the changes in agriculture and industry merit the description 'revolutionary'? Can the two revolutions really be compared? Am I right to include a 'political dimension' in the second revolution?

In attempting to answer questions like these, you'll have drawn attention to the importance of any such phrase used in future questions.

Answer

Guidance notes

In 1926, the Fifteenth Party Conference recorded the historic decision to begin 'the transformation of our country from an agrarian into an industrial one'. In accordance with this resolution, 'Stalin's economic policy had one essential aim, the modernisation of the Soviet Union, and two essential methods, collectivisation and industrialisation' (Lynch). To determine whether these policies may be justifiably described as a 'second revolution', it is necessary, firstly, to establish the facts – as opposed to the picture painted by Soviet propaganda – concerning these changes; secondly, to explore in more detail the motives behind the changes; thirdly, to compare the two Russian revolutions, particularly in regard to their successes and failures; and, lastly, to judge whether the appalling results of the changes can be vindicated by their historical necessity and whether alternative courses of action existed.

Introductions. A longer introduction, necessitated by the need to make clear the plan of the essay to come. Although you should not waste space on a 'wafflish' introduction, you must always make the plan of your answer clear. Here, the first sentence could be left out and the second shortened by putting the quotation in your own words.

In 1929, Stalin defined collectivisation as 'the setting up of *kolkhozy* [collective farms] and *sovkhozy* [state farms] in order

Quotations. A suitable quotation can be adapted to fit in a sentence by adding words of your own enclosed in **square brackets [...]**.

to squeeze out all capitalist elements from the land'. Both types of farm were to be the means by which 'private peasant-ownership was ended and agriculture was made to serve the interests of the Soviet state' (Lynch). By 1932 60% of all farmland was collectivised; by 1940 the figure had reached 97%. The kulaks – supposedly peasants grown rich under the NEP and now holding the workers to ransom – were the 'capitalist elements' which Stalin intended to 'squeeze out from the land', but their existence as a class has been revealed as a myth, although 'a very potent one [which] provided the pretext for the coercion of the peasantry as a whole' (Lynch). This coercion produced 'the first purely man-made famine in history'(Deutscher) and the deaths of ten to fifteen million peasants.

Paragraphs. The answer to **Question 6** in the introduction suggests that the **topic sentence** should normally be placed first. Here this has been done: the whole paragraph stresses the link between industrialisation and preparedness for war, with a final sentence summing up this theme and providing a **'link'** with the first sentence of the next paragraph.

War dominated Stalin's concept of Soviet industrialisation in the 1930s: just as he was waging war against the Soviet peasantry, so was he attempting to make the Soviet Union strong enough to resist attack from hostile capitalist powers. The first Five-Year Plan (FYP), from October 1928 to December 1932, concentrated on heavy industry, with consumer goods as a poor second; the second and third FYPs continued this trend with defence spending high during the 1930s (40% of the overall budget in 1933, 33% in 1940). But to call these plans is misleading: to designate targets without specifying the means of achieving them is hardly planning. 'Essentially the plan was a huge propaganda project' (Lynch) to bolster the idealism which inspired many of those who participated, to convince them that 'there is no fortress that we Bolsheviks cannot storm', and to justify low standards of living and harsh labour discipline in a nation under siege. By 1941 Soviet industrial workers were worse off than in 1928, but the USSR was in a position to fight and eventually to win World War Two.

The defeat of Nazi Germany has always been the chief argument put forward to justify the excesses of forced collectivisation and breakneck industrialisation. 'We are fifty or a hundred years behind the advanced countries', declared Stalin in 1931. 'We must make good this lag in ten years. Either we do it or they crush us.' But without the 'discontent with the compromises of the NEP ... the presentation of collectivisation, industrialisation and the so-called "cultural revolution" of the late 1920s, as class war ... [and the existence of] a new vanguard of the proletariat ... prepared to act as "shock troops"' (Bullock) support could not have been won from the middle and lower levels of the party.

Many were ready to reject Bukharin's alternative of 'making agriculture large-scale by implanting capitalism'; instead, as a Menshevik later wrote, they supported Stalin's methods of 'primitive socialist accumulation by the methods of Tamerlane'.

The October Revolution was an extraordinary success as a seizure of power by a minority party, led by a man who knew what he wanted. Marxism, however, provided little help in ruling a revolutionary state – hence the experiments with War Communism and the NEP, followed by the 'industrialisation debate' between left and right. Once Trotsky and the left were defeated, Stalin could afford to adopt its policies and carry them to extremes. Collectivisation cannot be justified on economic grounds, for Soviet agricultural productivity had barely returned to 1913 levels by 1939. If the awful human suffering which accompanied forced collectivisation is taken into account, it can only be seen as a staggering failure. Industrialisation was clearly more successful: 'the foundations of a major industrial power were laid during the first Five-Year Plan and completed during the second by 1939; it is estimated that total production was nearly four times higher than in 1928' (Bullock). But in both cases it is the scale of the changes – Stalin's obsession with 'gigantomania' – and even more the scale of the consequent suffering and social change which merit the title of the 'second revolution'.

Were there alternatives? Some have argued that Bukharin's policies would have succeeded with far less cost, but Bullock has shown that they were an alternative in principle but not in practice in the situation in the Soviet Union in 1928–9. Furthermore, the political dimension to this revolution must be stressed. Stalin reversed Marxism by claiming that the political system of a country should determine its economic system: 'building socialism' now meant using most unsocialistic methods. Thus dekulakisation could be completed and peasant resistance crushed in order to destroy the potentially hostile power of the largest class in the Soviet Union; centralised planning in industry similarly aided 'the building of a powerful state confronting a weak society' (Bullock).

With the addition of this political dimension, there can be no doubt that the 'second revolution' was indeed revolutionary.

Conclusions. Conclusions can be as short as this when much of the answer has already been covered in the preceding two paragraphs. Using one sentence in a paragraph always highlights its importance.

Mini essay plan

Paragraph 1	Introduction. Essential aims and methods of Stalin's economic policies.
Paragraph 2	Facts of collectivisation.
Paragraph 3	Facts of industrialisation.
Paragraph 4	Motives for these changes and the conditions necessary for party support.
Paragraph 5	The two revolutions compared.
Paragraph 6	The question of alternatives and the political dimension.
Paragraph 7	Conclusion. The 'second revolution' was revolutionary.

Related questions

1 What were Stalin's main objectives in embarking upon a policy of collectivisation and industrialisation?

2 'By 1933 the material conditions of the Soviet people had reached an unprecedently low level.' How far were Stalin's economic policies responsible for this situation?

3 'That the USSR was able to survive the war of 1941–5 was entirely due to Stalin's successful reconstruction of the Soviet economy by 1941.' Discuss.

General comments

The topic of the Soviet economy in the 1930s is obviously a 'must' in your **revision strategy**. To make sense of it, it's helpful to divide questions into the traditional three categories of **aims**, **methods** and **results**. The related questions include an example of each. Of course, **Questions 2 and 3** are also **relative importance** questions (requiring you to compare other factors responsible for the condition of the people in 2, and other causes of Soviet victory in World War Two in 3). The specimen essay focuses on the **results** of both policies and requires careful definition of the term 'second revolution'; further discussion on this and an alternative plan is given in **Lynch**, *Stalin and Khrushchev: the USSR 1924–64*.

You may, or may not, know much about economics, but some understanding of the subject is necessary if the history of the USSR in the 1920s and 1930s is to be understood. The A-level examiners will not expect a deep knowledge of economic theory, but they'll hope to find some awareness of the importance of economic factors in Soviet Russia. So, don't be afraid of questions with an economic slant; they're often easier than they look, if you've understood the basics.

Essay 11

'Stalinism was more than Stalinism: it was Leninism too.' Do you agree that the roots of Stalin's rule are discernible in Lenin's leadership of Soviet Russia?

Tackling the question

Now this one looks complicated, doesn't it? But don't be put off; like most long questions, it's easier than it looks. The actual question in the second sentence gives you more guidance than the quotation. In fact, it deals with another much discussed question: was there a straight line between Leninism and Stalinism and did one lead inevitably to the other?

Answer

Guidance notes

'Stalin is the Lenin of today.' Such slogans were commonplace during Stalin's rule; ever since his death and even before, historians were divided between those who saw a straight line joining Leninism and Stalinism and those who saw Stalin as 'not the executioner of Lenin's will but the executioner of Lenin's comrades' (Nove). To establish a balanced conclusion between views often diametrically opposed, it is necessary, first, to define both Leninism and Stalinism; secondly, to establish how different were the views of both men on economics, politics and foreign policy; thirdly, to consider the purges as an example of Stalinism in action; lastly, to attempt a conclusion which establishes some satisfying connection between the theory and practice of both men in power.

In exile, Lenin developed 'both the concept of a highly disciplined and centralised party and the notion of seizing power in a backward country and then creating the preconditions for socialism' (Nove). He saw how land-hungry peasants might be allied to the proletarian revolution, but also that party dictatorship would be necessary to revolutionise society from above. No other parties could be allowed; the crisis of the civil war might excuse the use of concentration camps, the secret police and the Red Terror, but they remained in place after the crisis was passed.

Introduction. Here the introduction sets out the necessary factors which must be considered for an answer to this question: definitions of both Leninism and Stalinism; the differences between both men on the major policy issues of the day; a consideration of the purges, possibly the most telling difference between them; finally, a conclusion which establishes how much of a connection there was between the theory and practice of both men. The reader is left in no doubt as to how you're going to tackle the question, and note the inclusion of a detailed paragraph on the purges to prevent the whole answer becoming too 'airy-fairy'.

Some writers advise you to include your actual answer to the question in the introduction; I would advise you to put it in your **mini essay plan** but not in your introduction. You should give the reader some incentive to get to the conclusion!

Rhetorical questions. You'll find that I use these fairly often, but not, I hope, too often. You should also restrain your use of them: they can become annoying for the reader if over-used. And don't forget to provide full answers for them!

Lenin might be personally modest and 'kind to secretaries, dogs and children', but it is hard to see his system leading to democracy in the Soviet Union – the history of that unhappy country shows how hard it is for democracy to take root there.

Stalinism might be described as a one-man despotism, using terror to destroy opposition and intimidate the people; a hierarchy of privilege with few rights for workers and poverty for peasants; the state having total control of the media and concerned only with 'socialism in one country', rather than with international revolution. 'Stalin's power was not based on control of the government, or the party or the political police. It involved exploiting all three ... Stalin was the only person in the entire country who saw the whole picture and he skilfully used the information available to him' (Martin McCauley).

Were collectivism and industrialisation a logical outcome of Leninism? At the end of his life, Lenin seemed ready to accept the continuation of the NEP and to support Bukharin's policy of gradualism and the conciliation of the peasants. Such a view is in direct contrast to Stalin's eventual espousal of forced collectivisation and rapid industrialisation, pleading the crisis of grain procurement and the external threat of the capitalist powers. Would Lenin have responded in the same way, if he had accepted that there was a crisis? The civil war had shown Lenin's ruthless side, but then the danger was obvious; it has been argued that in the 1930s Stalin was using a crisis that he had manufactured for his own advancement.

Stalin always stressed that he held power by the will of the party. During the 1930s, when his personal authority was established, he became answerable to no-one and had indeed 'become the Communist Party'. Whether dictatorship was always his goal has been debated: it seems likely that he reacted to each situation as it arose and had not carefully thought out a plan, although he did become convinced that only he could save the revolution from its enemies. Such thoughts might have occurred to Lenin, but as he was essentially modest in outlook it is very hard to see him in Stalin's role. However, to talk of 'the basically democratic nature of Leninism' may be wishful thinking; Alec Nove is nearer the mark when he writes of 'the despotic-dictatorial logic which can be seen as the essence of Leninism'. In foreign affairs, Stalin's 'socialism in one country' and the emasculation of the Comintern would seem difficult for Lenin, the international revolutionary, to have swallowed. But Trotsky's theory of 'permanent revolution' was already becoming unpopular before Lenin's death, and it is not too hard to imagine the abandonment of that policy and the concentration on building socialism in the one country where the revolution had succeeded.

It is in considering Stalin's purges that one is faced with the greatest difficulty in accepting the ideas of those who see a straight line joining Lenin to Stalin. The horrific numbers involved, the inexplicable attack on the armed forces when the country was in danger, the farcical nature of the show trials with their extraordinary confessions – all give weight to a belief in Stalin's paranoia and seem far from any scenario of which Lenin might have approved. The repression of 1922–3 pales into insignificance and can be partly excused by the pressures of a bloody and brutal civil war. Stalin's repression is of a different order and, moreover, aimed at Lenin's surviving comrades; it seems that all possible rivals must be eliminated before they can begin to think of treachery. By no means were all the casualties Stalin's direct responsibility, but there is no doubt of his overall control.

Punctuation. Here the **dash** is used to sum up a list of three separate points about the purges.

Robert Tucker sees 'NEP society ... [as] ... an interval of relative quiescence between two phases of the Russian revolutionary process: the 1917–21 phase ... and the Stalinist phase that ensued in 1929–39'. He finds Lenin distinguishing the 'revolutionary approach' (War Communism) from the 'reformist approach' (the NEP) and envisaging 'the involvement of the entire population in cooperative forms of work ... [after] ... a gradual long-range "cultural revolution"' had ensured their 'voluntary acceptance of cooperative socialism'. Thus, he claims, the Bukharinist 'reformist' alternative was inspired by Lenin's thinking towards the end of his life and, as Moshe Lewin has claimed, would have worked better than the Stalinist 'revolutionary' alternative. In other words, the link between Stalinism and Leninism depends on which Lenin one quotes: either Lenin's last writings, which he intended to be his political testament, or the whole of his lifetime's thought and writing, in which Stalin could claim to find support for his 'revolution from above', with the agreement of Bolsheviks of his own generation 'who politically came of age ... during the era of War Communism'. There were, indeed, echoes of Stalinism in Lenin's thoughts and actions, but his last writings indicate that he foresaw a very different socialist future to that constructed by his successor.

Essay 11

Mini essay plan

Paragraph 1	Introduction. Was there a straight line joining Lenin to Stalin?
Paragraph 2	An outline of Leninism.
Paragraph 3	... and of Stalinism.
Paragraph 4	Were collectivisation and industrialisation a logical outcome of Leninism?
Paragraph 5	Leninism not democratic in outlook, but it is hard to see the modest Lenin in Stalin's dictatorial role.
Paragraph 6	Lenin might have come to support 'socialism in one country' when Trotsky's 'permanent revolution' proved impossible.
Paragraph 7	The Stalinist purges show his repression to be of a different order to that carried out by Lenin.
Paragraph 8	Conclusion. There are echoes of Stalinism in Lenin's thought and writing, and in his actions, but his last writings indicate a different political testament.

General comments

Related questions

1 What was the significance of the murder of Kirov in 1934?

2 'The real puzzle is not why Stalin conducted a policy of terror, but why the Soviet Union accepted it.' Discuss.

3 How acceptable is the view that 'the purges strengthened Stalin personally, but weakened the Soviet Union nationally'?

Apart from questions on links between the policies of Lenin and Stalin, the most likely topic for consideration concerning Stalin's exercise of power is the whole story of the purges. As **Michael Lynch** points out, the important issues here are Stalin's motives, his means of achieving them and the lack of resistance to those methods. He discusses a possible answer to **Question 1**.

Question 2 links motives and the lack of resistance. **Question 3** deals with another obvious issue to add to the list: the results of the purges, both for Stalin and the USSR.

It is clearly helpful to divide possible questions into such issues; the paragraphs required for the answers will be more apparent and you will be encouraged when you recognise them in the exam paper. You'll be glad to hear that the examiners have relatively few different types of question which they can ask on most topics; if you're aware of these types, you can prepare to answer the likely questions more easily.

Essay 12

'The USSR signed the treaty with Nazi Germany in 1939 not out of choice but out of necessity.' Discuss.

Tackling the question

The second foreign policy essay. Although the quotation focuses on one event (the Nazi–Soviet Pact of August 1939), it covers the whole of Soviet foreign policy from 1924 to 1939. Always be on the look-out for these questions, for it is fair to say that any which name one event will always require you to analyse events either before or after; sometimes a long way before, as in this case.

Answer

Guidance notes

The announcement of the Nazi–Soviet Pact on 24 August 1939 was a bombshell for the West. To determine whether the Soviet Union had any choice of allies in 1939 and how essential such allies were for her national safety, it is necessary to examine the course of Soviet foreign policy from 1924 to 1939, paying due respect to the long history of Russo-German co-operation and to the international reaction to the rise of Nazi power in Germany.

When Lenin died, the Treaty of Rapallo was firmly established as the basis of Soviet foreign policy. What Kochin calls 'the adjustment of revolution to the standards and attitudes of capitalist diplomacy' was under way. The hope of world revolution had been temporarily abandoned and Lenin's policy of 'exploiting contradictions' in the capitalist world had replaced it. 'The German bourgeois Government madly hates the Bolsheviks,' Lenin admitted, 'but the interests of its international position impel it towards peace with Soviet Russia against its own wish.' The Soviet government was similarly impelled towards Germany since the 'contradictions' between the victorious Allies and their defeated enemy were the most obvious ones to exploit. Rapallo became 'the sheet anchor of Russian foreign policy'. There was great concern when Germany

Factual evidence. This paragraph concerns the **Treaty of Rapallo**. I've not given its details, thus assuming that the reader knows them. Do you think that this is correct in this case? If in doubt, you should play for safety and give the details as briefly as possible.

Paragraphs. Note how the first sentence makes clear the position in 1929; what follows describes Soviet foreign policy during the 1930s. In an account of a sequence of events, it is always helpful to put in one or two **'signposts'** which sum up the position so far.

Technical terms. *Rapprochement* is a useful word in dealing with foreign policy, but be sure that you know exactly what it means. The dictionary definition ('the re-establishment of cordial relations, particularly between nations') stresses that these relations once existed and have again been established.

Style. Beware of using modern or slang phrases. Examiners often refer to this in their reports and criticise some candidates for adopting them. **'U-turn'** has now become accepted as a useful phrase, but many others have not. Remember that you should be on your best literary behaviour when writing an essay!

threatened *rapprochement* with the western powers by her signature of the Locarno agreements, but Rapallo was reaffirmed in the Treaty of Berlin (1926) and there were important German–Soviet trade treaties in 1925 and 1931.

By 1929, the Soviet Union was accepted as a member of the international community and the capitalist world was threatened with economic disaster. But in the Soviet Union, fear was growing that Germany was becoming too powerful: when she attempted a customs union with Austria in 1931, 'Moscow saw the amber light' (Kochin). Now Stalin and Litvinov began to seek a *rapprochement* with France and Poland – pacts were made with both in 1932 – for they were still faithful to Lenin's policy of 'supporting one group of capitalist powers against another'. Hitler, not Stalin, finally ended the Rapallo alliance when he concluded a non-aggression pact with Poland in 1934 – the threat of German aggression was now much nearer Soviet borders. Before 1933, Stalin had encouraged the KPD to co-operate with the Nazis; afterwards he was too late to organise the German centre and left against the Nazi menace. For the next five years, Stalin attempted to find allies against Germany and to buy off the Japanese threat in the east – in 1935 with the sale of the Chinese Eastern Railway at a knock-down price. Soviet foreign policy would now embrace collective security and a strong League, which she joined in 1934.

It is hard to see any alternative to the 'U-turn' in Soviet policy which followed the break with Germany. Determined not to be isolated, and faced with a challenge on two fronts from Germany and Japan – achieving a final menacing form in the Anti-Comintern Pact of 1936 – the Soviet Union could hope to find safety only in alliance with the capitalist powers, which appeared ready to control Hitler through collective security and the League. But the existence of the Comintern – even though it was now appealing for an anti-fascist Popular Front in Europe – made Britain and France suspicious of Stalin's intentions; they could not forget the 'twin-track approach of attempting to foment revolution in those countries with which the USSR had regular diplomatic relations' (Condren), which had been seen as normal by the Soviet government since the 1920s. Similarly, Stalin found Britain and France more and more drawn towards appeasement as Germany, Italy and Japan all enlarged their territories in the 1930s without any effective action from the League. The Spanish Civil War finally 'bankrupted collective security' (Overy) and the

Munich Conference – to which Stalin was not invited in spite of his treaty links with Czechoslovakia – was the last straw in his disillusionment with that ill-fated policy. Critics in the West might view Munich as the climax of appeasement; for Stalin, it had all the signs of a conspiracy to allow Germany a free hand to attack an isolated Soviet Union. Between March and August 1939 the Soviet Union found itself courted by both sides. Stung into action by Hitler's occupation of Czechoslovakia, the British and French gave a guarantee to Poland against German aggression; they soon came to realise that such a guarantee would be militarily feasible only with Soviet assistance. But their reluctance to trust Stalin meant that Soviet proposals for a formal alliance were disregarded and not until 12 August were military talks begun. By then it was too late. The Germans had started to explore the possibility of close relations in April; in May Litvinov was replaced by Molotov – a Soviet nationalist more pro-German than pro-West; on 30 May, the German ambassador was instructed 'to undertake definite negotiations with the Soviet Union'. On 29 August the Nazi–Soviet Pact was signed and Hitler was able to launch his planned attack on Poland.

Ribbentrop had made Stalin an offer he could not refuse. Britain and France, long distrusted, could propose no more than participation in an immediate European war, with the Soviet army still reeling from the effects of the purges. Germany offered the Soviet Union neutrality in that capitalist war and a breathing space to prepare for the expected German attack. There was no real choice here: the Nazi–Soviet Pact represents a 'rational, even a predictable' policy for the Soviets, with the recognition of ingrained western appeasement 'and the obvious military weakness of Britain' (Overy). Soviet foreign policy, unlike that of the tsars, had always been defensive; now was not the moment to be drawn into war with a powerful Germany.

Essay 12

Mini essay plan

Paragraph 1 — Introduction. Did the Soviets have a choice of allies in 1939 and how necessary were such allies?

Paragraph 2 — Soviet foreign policy, 1922–9.

Paragraph 3 — Soviet foreign policy, 1929–34.

Paragraph 4 — Soviet foreign policy, 1934–9.

Paragraph 5 — Conclusion. The pact with Germany was an offer which Stalin could not refuse. There was no real choice between what Germany and the West offered, since peace was essential to give a breathing space after the purges.

Related questions

1 How consistent was Soviet foreign policy in the period 1924–39?

2 How and why did Soviet foreign policy change during the 1930s?

3 How far do you consider Stalin's foreign policy was a cause of the outbreak of war in September 1939?

General comments

You can divide examination questions on foreign policy into **two main types**: those dealing with a particular event (often involving its long-term causes and results) and those which try to sum up the policy over a period.

Question 1 is obviously of the latter type. **'Consistent'** is a favourite word in such questions; any judgement on consistency must involve a clear statement of the **aims of foreign policy** over a period. In this case you could stress the defensive character of Soviet policy.

Question 2 is of the same type, using the favourite **'how and why'** formula, and focusing on the 'U-turns' in the 1930s.

Question 3 is concerned with a particular event (the outbreak of World War Two), but like the specimen essay, it reaches back into the diplomatic moves of the 1930s. It is also, of course, a **relative importance** question, which will require plenty of detail on the alternative causes of World War Two.

essay questions

Fascist
Italy

Essay 1

'The socialist threat and the weakness of postwar liberal governments enabled fascism to grow and achieve power in 1922.' Discuss.

Tackling the question

Now we shift to the study of Mussolini's Italy. The rise to power of the Duce and his party is the first and most obvious of the questions on this period. Here we have a **long question**, using an apparently complex quotation. Careful analysis will show that four factors are involved: two named causes of the growth of fascism and its achievement of power in 1922. As the introduction points out, the socialist threat was one obvious cause of the growth of fascism between 1919 and 1922 (what were the others?), while the weakness of the liberal government in 1922 was equally a cause of fascism's triumph, although the essay will explore the part played by Mussolini's leadership and the actions of the king. Thus we have a **double relative importance** question. Note also that the causes of the growth of fascism may, or may not, also be the causes of its success in 1922.

Answer

Guidance notes

The causes of the growth of fascism are already apparent by the end of World War One. To estimate the importance of the socialist threat, all these causes must be weighed in considering the early history of the movement, between 1919 and 1921. To understand how Mussolini achieved power in 1922, it is important to look beyond the admitted weakness of the liberal governments and focus particularly on Mussolini's leadership and the actions of the king.

A. de Grand sees the First World War as marking 'a rupture in the course of Italian political development', pushing Italy from 'instability to crisis' (Lee). Such instability had been present since unification – 38 ministries held office between 1860 and 1922 – with governments depending on the corrupt *trasformismo* system. Peace produced economic strains and the threat of social disruption. Italy's war expenditure was more than twice the total

Technical terms. You must be fully familiar with the *trasformismo* system; do you think that I should have included a definition of it? One way of deciding is to ask yourself how important for the whole argument in the essay is the phrase in question. Where it is central to that argument, the case for definition becomes much stronger.

expenditure of all Italian governments since 1861; she was left with a vast national debt, rampant inflation and soaring unemployment. The urban and rural working classes feared further decline in their standard of living, industrialists and landowners would not increase wages or lower rents, while an impoverished lower middle class distrusted both capital and labour.

Political divisions widened as the economy worsened. Industrial workers pushed membership of the Socialist Party (PSI) to about 200,000 by 1919. In the elections of that year, they won 156 seats, with 32.4% of the popular vote – a party dedicated to violent revolution was now the largest group in the Italian parliament. A predominantly Catholic party, the PPI, had emerged on the Right and political stability could only be achieved by a coalition of these two major parties. But they were irreconcilable. Liberal governments struggled on, but they were quite unable to head off the crisis between capital and labour and were eventually driven to depend on the fascists to take violent action against unions and peasant leagues.

Another threat to the liberal hold on power emerged after the peace treaties had provided no more than a 'mutilated victory'. Nationalists blamed the liberals for failing to gain more territory around the Adriatic and a share of the German colonies in Africa. Demobilised soldiers felt betrayed by the peace terms and were ready to support the dynamic nationalism of the fascists. D'Annunzio, at Fiume, had shown the way, and his fondness for drama and publicity was not lost on another enemy of liberalism, Benito Mussolini.

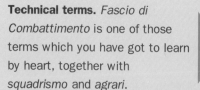

'With the war over and the socialists in the ascendant, Mussolini the socialist renegade lay stranded on the margin of political life' (Blinkhorn). He had founded the *Fascio di Combattimento* in March 1919, but his challenge to the socialists for working-class support – on a programme that was republican, anti-clerical and anti-business – in the elections of 1919 was a disaster. No seats were won and the survival of the new movement was in the balance. It was rescued by 'the government's failure to convince conservative Italians that it could deal with the supposed socialist threat' (Robson). Fiume, factory occupations, agrarian strikes and land occupations, the success of the socialists in the local government elections in 1920 – all persuaded industrialists,

Technical terms. The use of initials for Italian and German parties is obviously a useful abbreviation; giving the full name of the party on the first occasion that you use it is equally impressive (if you can remember and spell it!). Be sure you don't get the initials muddled, though.

Technical terms. *Fascio di Combattimento* is one of those terms which you have got to learn by heart, together with *squadrismo* and *agrari*.

landowners, war veterans and the urban middle class that the liberal government – now led by Giolitti, the great champion of *trasformismo* – would do nothing to save them from that socialist threat. To stave off the coming revolution, they were ready to employ fascist squads eager to fight socialists. Violence continued into the spring of 1921 and Mussolini had to fight hard to preserve his leadership of a movement where local Ras – such as Balbo in Ferrara and Dino Grandi in Bologna – were unwilling to surrender their independent power. He co-operated with Giolitti in the election of 1921, which gave the fascists 7% of the popular vote and 35 seats in parliament, and made fascism into a political party (PFI), while continuing to appeal to the conservatives by stressing opposition to socialists and liberals and playing down the violence of the *squadrismo*. By the end of 1921, the new party had 200,000 members.

Within a year, Mussolini was prime minister. 'During 1922 the conviction formed in political circles, within the Vatican and the Catholic hierarchy, among 'liberal' intellectuals and journalists, and among industrialists and *agrari*, that fascism must be given its political chance' (Blinkhorn). In the spring, fascists fought openly in the streets of northern Italian cities and were able to defeat a general strike called by the Socialists in August. By October, plans for a march on Rome were being laid and with fascists mobilising in the provinces, Facta asked the king to declare martial law and order the army to suppress the expected march. Agreeing at first, the king then changed his mind; Facta resigned and Mussolini was appointed premier on 29 October.

Factual evidence. Does this paragraph give enough detail on the events of 1922? If not, what would you add? Where you're dealing with the amount of detail to include in a paragraph describing events, you should be asking yourself all the time whether you have included sufficient detail or burdened the reader and wasted valuable space and time with too much.

There can be no doubt that the socialist threat greatly enhanced conservative support for Mussolini, just as the weakness of successive Liberal governments and their eventual decision to co-operate with the PNF opened the way for him to achieve power. But the fascists appeared to offer more than a merely anti-socialist programme, and they had a leader who knew how to propagate a new, energetic and exciting programme. Moreover, it must be remembered that it was the king, for whatever reasons, who refused Facta's demand to disperse the marchers by force and thus gave Mussolini his chance to bluff his way into power, rather than face the almost certain ignominy of the failure of the blackshirt threat to Rome and the consequent puncturing of the myth of fascist power.

Essay 1

Mini essay plan

Paragraph 1 Introduction. The causes of the growth of fascism are already apparent in 1918: the socialist threat must be weighed against other factors in the period 1919–21, while the actions of the king in October 1922 are important for Mussolini's achievement of power.

Paragraph 2 The effects of World War One.

Paragraph 3 The widening of political divisions as the economy worsens.

Paragraph 4 The effect of a 'mutilated victory'.

Paragraph 5 Early history of the Fascist Party, 1919–21.

Paragraph 6 The events of 1922.

Paragraph 7 Conclusion. The socialist threat and the weakness of successive liberal governments were important, but the fact that the fascists offered more than a merely anti-socialist programme and that it was the actions of the king which made the March on Rome a success were both of greater importance.

Related questions

1 Mussolini was an opportunist. How far does this explain his rise to power by 1922?

2 Examine the means by which Mussolini achieved power in 1922. How did he seek to strengthen his position in the next seven years?

3 Examine the view that the primary cause of Mussolini's rise to power in the early 1920s was the effect of World War One on the Italian people.

General comments

Here are typical questions on Mussolini's rise to power. **Question 1** focuses on his conduct during the period. An answer would stress his lack of principle, but must also stress the other causes of his success. **Remember that there's a great temptation in writing an answer to this type of question to concentrate too much on the named cause.**

Question 2 is typical of those questions – found particularly in Outlines papers – which go beyond 1922 to examine the strengthening of Mussolini's position after he gained power.

Question 3 again picks out one cause of Mussolini's success, even though that cause itself has different characteristics. Other causes must still be examined in your answer.

Essay 2

How totalitarian was Mussolini's rule in Italy?

Tackling the question

Here is a really short question! You can see how you're going to have to provide the plan of the answer without any help from the question. Obviously, there must be a definition of **'totalitarian'** in your plan (and there has been much debate about this, so be careful!) and the various aspects of the fascist state must be examined. A useful book here is *Fascist Italy* *and Nazi Germany -- the 'Fascist' Style of Rule*, by **Alexander J. De Grand**, in the Historical Connections series, published by Routledge. This not only provides many similarities and differences between fascist and Nazi rule, but also serves as an excellent short account of the rise to power of Hitler and Mussolini and the functioning of their respective states.

Answer

Guidance notes

The concept of totalitarianism, first formulated by the Italian philosopher and fascist Giovanni Gentile in 1925, has been much criticised since its widespread use in the propaganda battles of the Cold War. Definition is necessary before examining the structures of the fascist state – in its political, economic, social and foreign policy aspects – both in theory and practice, to see how nearly it accords with the totalitarian model.

The best known formulation of the 'totalitarian syndrome' is that produced by Friedrich and Brzezinski in 1950. It had six features: an official ideology, a single mass party typically led by one man, a monopoly of control of the armed forces and over the means of mass communication, a system of police control using terror and, finally, the central control and direction of the entire economy. In spite of its weaknesses (its static nature and exaggeration of the monolithic nature of totalitarian regimes) it remains the most useful description of such regimes.

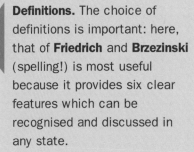

Definitions. The choice of definitions is important: here, that of **Friedrich** and **Brzezinski** (spelling!) is most useful because it provides six clear features which can be recognised and discussed in any state.

Essay 2

Punctuation. Note the **dash** used to sum up a long list of **'if's'**...

How did Mussolini envisage the fascist Italy that he wished to construct? In 1932 he defined the basic ideas of the fascist movement in his *Political and Social Doctrine of Fascism*, describing it as anti-communist and anti-socialist, anti-democratic, authoritarian ('Fascism conceives of the state as an absolute') and promoting territorial expansion and war as 'an essential manifestation of vitality'. But the book also contains 'a hotchpotch of the ideas of conflicting sub-movements and sub-ideologies', syndicalism, conservatism and nationalism among them. Such a wide range of conflicting ideas might be an advantage in the struggle to gain power but was equally a disadvantage in setting up a fascist state – Mussolini himself admitted that 'Fascism ... was not a doctrine but a technique; it was a means to gain power' (Mack Smith). The contradictions involved in such a state might be obvious, but if it were sufficiently authoritarian, if all opposition in parliament could be crushed and parliament itself disregarded and finally replaced, if the Fascist Party were brought under central control by an acknowledged leader, if powerful interests (the king, the army, the church, the civil service, the conservative leaders of industry and agriculture, the workers in field and factory) could be bought off or otherwise persuaded to support the regime and the cult of Il Duce – then power gained by opportunism might become the basis of a new Italy.

A considerable part of the former political structure was left intact, particularly the power of the local Prefects. Parliament's power was gradually eliminated between 1923 and 1939. Control of the Fascist Party was centralised in the Fascist Grand Council, under Mussolini's command, but it played little part in policy decisions. In January 1926 Mussolini was empowered to govern by decree; he was now personally responsible for eight key ministries. This impossible workload led to extraordinary administrative inefficiency, but Mussolini was intent on ruling by balancing the different elements which might challenge his authority – as Lee remarks, he was 'deliberately creating a vacuum in the political and administrative structure ... which was filled by the "cult of the Duce"'. Thus 'the Fascist political dictatorship was only half implemented ... Mussolini introduced new institutions but then refused to let them function properly in order to protect his own popular image'.

In economic policy, the most obvious innovation was the Corporate State – the fascist alternative to socialism and capitalism. But the whole system was 'inefficient and cumbersome and was almost entirely excluded from any real decision-making in the economy' (Lee). Financial policies were often dictated by considerations of national prestige – notably in the fixing of too high a value of the lira. In industry, large private companies were at first untouched, but later the IRI extended government control in pursuit of *autarky*. The 'Battle for Grain' might be won in agriculture, but only at the expense of other, more suitable, crops. The Pontine Marshes and other reclamation schemes might provide more arable land, but *autarky* 'remained just a pipe dream ... the Italian economy was not ready for war in 1940' (Robson).

Unlike Hitler and Stalin, Mussolini was never personally cruel, and his more fragile hold over the Italian people would never have allowed him to indulge in mass purges or to set up mass concentration camps. But he did believe in 'surgical violence' against enemies (his three most prominent opponents were all assassinated) although the OVRA could never compare with the Gestapo in terror tactics – 'the fascist regime used terror, but was not in any real sense based on terror' (Cassels). Indoctrination, at first in education, later in youth groups, had some success among the young, but there was inefficiency in and resistance to the spreading of the message, although Mussolini retained his personal popularity. Control of the press and propaganda was more successful, but even here there was a price to pay – 'propaganda as a substitute for action ... [was] ... almost the essence of fascism' (Mack Smith).

Violence and propaganda also ruled in foreign affairs. The use of poison gas in Libya and Ethiopia, the destruction of whole villages in both countries, the execution of anti-fascist prisoners in Spain – all show the ugly face of fascism relieved of the inhibitions imposed at home. Similarly, propaganda always overcame truth, particularly in Mussolini's bombastic claims that Italy had 'five million bayonets', that her air force would 'darken the sun' and that Italy herself was 'one big aircraft carrier'.

It can thus be seen that 'between 1922 and 1943 Mussolini established, at least in theory, all the institutions and devices associated with the totalitarian state' (Lee). But Martin Clark finds the regime's claims to totalitarianism 'laughable ... there was acceptance but not devotion, consensus but not commitment'. In Italy's case, 'totalitarianism was a dream so far short of accomplishment as to invalidate the entire approach' (Blinkhorn).

Technical terms. *Autarky* is an important term used in dealing with the economic policies of both fascist Italy and Nazi Germany. A useful source for definitions of core concepts (although not, unfortunately, *autarky*) can be found in *The Good History Students' Handbook*, edited by **Gilbert Pleuger** (Sempringham); fairly elementary books on politics will also be a possible source.

Conclusions. You may think that this conclusion is too full of quotations. Try putting the sense of it in your own words, using the minimum of quotation.

Essay 2

Mini essay plan

Paragraph 1	Introduction. Definition of totalitarianism essential before examining the structure of the fascist state.
Paragraph 2	Definition of totalitarianism.
Paragraph 3	Mussolini's fascist state in theory.
Paragraph 4	The fascist state in practice: the political structure.
Paragraph 5	Economic policy: the Corporate State.
Paragraph 6	Social policy: indoctrination, violence and propaganda.
Paragraph 7	Foreign affairs: violence and propaganda again.
Paragraph 8	Conclusion. In theory, a totalitarian state; in practice, the claim is laughable and a dream.

Related questions

1 Why was Mussolini able both to obtain office and to consolidate his power in Italy during the years 1922 to 1929?

2 Compare the regimes of the Duce and the Führer.

3 What success had Mussolini's Corporate State in solving Italy's economic and social problems?

General comments

Three types of popular question on the establishment and working of the fascist regime are given here. **Question 1** focuses partly on Mussolini's consolidation of power in Italy after 1922. As with all **double questions**, the secret of success is in the **balance** accorded to the two parts in your answer.

Question 2 concerns the comparison between the fascist and Nazi states. As in all such questions, the temptation is to write one half of the answer on one part and one half on the other. **Resist this temptation!** You must fix on certain attributes of these states and write a paragraph on each, setting out the points of similarity and difference between the two systems. A final paragraph before your conclusion should summarise these.

Question 3 is typical of the sort of question which deals with the success of a particular system in solving certain problems (these might equally have been described as those which brought Mussolini to power). Your answer must define the problems, describe the solutions and judge their success.

Essay 3

By what stages and for what reasons did Mussolini move from accord with Britain and France to alliance with Germany and entry into World War Two?

Tackling the question

A longer, **double question**, on foreign policy. This illustrates the typical type of question dealing with foreign policy over an extended period, sometimes set as the change from one situation to another, as in this case. As usual, the question of **balance** will be vital for success.

Answer

Guidance notes

There has been considerable debate among historians about the motives for Mussolini's foreign policy, but the events of the period, it is generally agreed, fall naturally into three phases: 1922–33, 1933–6 and 1936–40. Accordingly, this essay will examine both the aims and events of Italian policy during these three periods before providing a conclusion covering the whole period.

Introductions. Here, the introduction divides the period into three phases, chosen by the author. This is just the sort of decision which should have been made during your revision; to arrive at a sensible division in the heat of an exam is particularly difficult.

It seems clear that in 1922 Mussolini had no definite foreign policy beyond the general aim of making Italy 'great, respected and feared'. As the 1920s progressed, it became apparent that 'the domination of Europe by France and Britain precluded not merely an aggressively revisionist foreign policy but also the kind of international equilibrium necessary for Italy to enjoy diplomatic importance as a potential upsetter of the balance of power' (Blinkhorn). Thus Mussolini's policy was erratic during the period: aggression alternated with conciliation, verbal defiance of the status quo with the desire for 'acceptance as a "respectable" statesman of continental stature', hostility to France and subversive attempts to undermine her 'Little Entente' in south-east Europe with signature of the Locarno and Kellogg Pacts. By the late 1920s, Mussolini was becoming impatient with

Essay 3

Paragraphs. It is often useful to include several sentences of detailed description of an event in order to illustrate a general point which is being made. Apart from anything else, it will show your detailed knowledge of the subject, always a good thing to impress on the examiner! But it will help a lot to have thought it out before you come to the exam.

the lack of success from this unfocused and opportunist policy, his language became increasingly belligerent and, from 1928, revisionism of the 'mutilated victory' became official policy.

The occupation of the Greek island of Corfu well illustrates Mussolini's approach to foreign affairs in this first phase – a blustering response to a minor incident; demands that the Greek government were unlikely to meet; military occupation of the island; unwilling acceptance of a compromise (soon turned by propaganda into a victory) under strong diplomatic pressure, particularly from Britain. He was more successful in bullying Yugoslavia into relinquishing Fiume (Pact of Rome, 1924). Under some pressure from British diplomats and the Italian Foreign Ministry, he signed the Locarno Pact and appeared to many in Britain and France to be forsaking force for a more moderate stance. But his deep dislike of France, 'partly ideological ... partly strategic', led him to an unsuccessful attempt to detach Yugoslavia from the French-dominated 'Little Entente'.

For Mussolini, the European situation was entirely changed by Hitler's coming to power in 1933. Now that Germany represented an alternative power-bloc to the Anglo-French alliance, he could abandon the latter and become a possible neutral mediator between the two, with hope of concessions from both. Alternatively, alliance with Germany was an obvious means of putting pressure on Britain and France, again with the hope of Italian gains. The threat of Austrian *Anschluss* after Dollfuss' assassination might lead to temporary alliance in the 'Stresa Front', but this only encouraged Mussolini to embark on his Ethiopian adventure with the confident and correct anticipation that his new allies would make no serious attempts to stop him.

Britain and France indeed proved to be 'paper tigers' in defence of Ethiopia. The popular reaction against the Hoare–Laval Pact and the ineffective sanctions imposed by the League on Italy (excluding vital war materials such as oil, and without the closure of the Suez Canal) did nothing to halt the victory which made Mussolini the most popular leader in Italy's short history. But the results were vital. Britain and France were never to trust Italy again; Hitler was beginning to emerge as the chief threat to European peace, Mussolini might boast of the 'century of fascism' to come, but Italy was being driven inexorably into the 'brutal friendship' (Deakin) with Germany which was to lead her to disaster.

'From 1936 the accommodation with Germany was the essential fact of Italian foreign policy' (Robson). Italy's intervention in the Spanish Civil War sprang partly from Mussolini's hatred of the Popular Front Government, but also from the use a friendly fascist Spain might be in making Gibraltar more vulnerable and weakening Britain's naval strategy in the Mediterranean. The results were disastrous. Franco showed little gratitude and the losses in men and materials could not be made up by 1939, leaving Mussolini unable to join Germany in the Second World War until 1940. Britain and France abandoned hope of friendship with Italy and began to rearm at a pace she could not match, pushing her ever closer to Germany. In February 1939 Mussolini told the Fascist Grand Council that Italy was 'a prisoner of the Mediterranean ... the bars of this prison are Corsica, Tunis, Malta, Cyprus ... the sentinels of this prison are Gibraltar and Suez ... the task of Italian policy ... is to first of all break the bars of the prison'. But such grandiloquent plans were now dependent on the German alliance for success.

Events moved fast from 1936 onwards. While Italy tried out her armed forces in Spain and occupied Albania, Hitler was uniting Germany with Austria, taking the Sudeten lands (after Munich, where Mussolini made his last appearance as an international mediator), occupying the remainder of Czechoslovakia, and signing the Nazi–Soviet Pact – all without reference to his Italian ally. Bound more closely to the might of Germany by the Pact of Steel, Mussolini was, to his shame, unable to join Hitler in his attack on Poland, and did not declare war on France and England until June 1940.

Some historians have seen Mussolini's expansionist policies in the 1930s as a response to domestic failures; others find an underlying consistency, with revisionism and expansion providing the prime inspiration for Mussolini's actions. Although the former explanation contains some truth, it was the latter policy which inevitably brought Italy into conflict with Britain and France, making the fatal alliance with Nazi Germany equally inescapable.

Conclusions. It is usually better to name the historians whose views you're describing, but it is not vital to do so. **Stephen Lee** provides examples from the books of those who see Mussolini's foreign policy as designed to 'mobilise popular support and maintain domestic harmony through the deliberate use of aggressive diplomacy, territorial expansion and war' (not least **Mack Smith**, who agrees that the purpose of Mussolini's foreign policy was to bolster his prestige).

The opposite view is taken by **Martin Blinkhorn** who states that 'there is little doubt that revisionism did constitute the prime inspiration for Mussolini's behaviour in the international arena' ('revisionism' meaning the desire to alter the Versailles treaty in Italy's favour).

Note that conclusions can be shortened by not naming the historians, particularly, as in this case, when the last sentence brings the argument back to the question itself.

Essay 3

General comments

Related questions

1 How successful had Mussolini been in achieving the aims of his foreign policy by the end of 1940?

2 'Any history of Mussolini's foreign policy has to be ... a history of propaganda.' How far do you agree with this judgement?

3 'Fascism in Italy relied on publicity and propaganda rather than on solid achievement.' Discuss.

Question 1 is the usual question on 'success in achieving aims', although you must be careful to notice the date '1940'. **Question 2** concentrates on the use of propaganda in Italian foreign policy of this period and is in line with those who see it as essentially tied in with domestic policy. **Question 3** is a general question on Mussolini's rule in which foreign policy plays an important role.

essay questions

Nazi Germany

Essay 1

'Perhaps the greatest piece of good fortune in my life.' Do you agree with Hitler's judgement on the Munich Putsch of 1923?

Tackling the question

Here is the most obvious example of a **question on a single event**: the Munich Putsch lasted less than 24 hours. But although some space must be given to those hours (and even more to a description of the situation in Bavaria and in Germany as a whole during 1923), the Hitler quotation also requires you to examine the years after the putsch, at least as far as 1928. Any A-level question based on a single event will inevitably need discussion on long periods **before and after** it occurred.

Answer

Guidance notes

It is tempting to dismiss this comment of Hitler's on his most obvious political blunder as an attempt to justify failure with his usual rhetoric. To test the truth of his statement, it is necessary to examine the situation in Germany – and particularly in Bavaria – in 1923, the events of the putsch and the conduct of Hitler during those 24 hours, and then to estimate the consequences of his failure during the rest of the 1920s.

1923 was a year of crisis for the new Republic. In January the French occupied the Ruhr in order to end German prevarication over the payment of reparations. The mark collapsed, bringing great suffering, particularly on the middle classes. North Germany experienced a quickly suppressed military putsch, a separatist movement in the Rhineland was growing, the left was making headway in Saxony and Thuringia – 'a revolutionary situation had arisen charged with moods and expectations of civil war' (Fest). Hitler was well aware of the chance that such a situation offered in the unstable condition of Bavaria, with a growing tide of opposition to the Berlin government. That opposition was divided between the monarchist followers of

Paragraphs. As full an account as possible of the situation in Germany, and particularly in Bavaria, is required, before describing the events of 8/9 November. This will need a longish paragraph, as here, but be careful not to get carried away! Once again, planning of such a paragraph before the exam will pay dividends; it's unlikely that you'll produce a good one under pressure without prior thought.

General State Commissioner von Kahr, the various 'Fighting Leagues' grouped around Ludendorff and Hitler's NSDAP, more than 55,000 strong. All discussed a 'march on Red Berlin' (Mussolini's March on Rome was an example to be followed) but their only point of agreement was that 'in no circumstances would any of the three leave action to their rivals'. By September, the new government in Berlin, led by Stresemann, had abandoned resistance to the French in the Ruhr while Hitler was calling for 'a march on Berlin and the installation of a national dictatorship', but such a move was obviously dependent on the support of the Bavarian government and the Reichswehr, as well as that of the Kampfbund. When the NSDAP and the SA were deliberately excluded from the planning of the march on Berlin, Hitler feared that the Bavarian government might act without him. Time was running out: the Berlin government, backed by von Seeckt and the Reichswehr, could soon have the situation under control. On 6 November, he decided to act on his own – not from strength, but as 'the last desperate gamble of a man who feared he was being deserted by his fellow-conspirators'.

Paragraphs. Similarly, don't write too much on the actual events of the putsch. Note that this is actually the shortest paragraph in the essay.

When the time came for decisive action on the evening of 8 November, Hitler 'proved singularly ineffective'. Receiving no more than unwilling support, at pistol point, from the Bavarian leaders at the Bürgerbräukeller, he unwisely left them with Ludendorff, who allowed them to leave and begin efforts to suppress the coup. On discovering this, Hitler suffered a nervous collapse until persuaded by Ludendorff to march on the following day. By then he had probably lost faith in the whole enterprise, and although it is unlikely that he was guilty of cowardice when faced by armed police, the outcome left no doubt that the whole unplanned coup had ended in disaster.

Questions. I hope you have remembered to approach these specimen essays with an inquiring mind. I shall be noting some of the questions you might be considering in future essays: here, it's worth asking yourself whether the putsch was as much of a gamble as it appears. Certainly it came too late and was marred by serious errors of judgement, but it's interesting to note that **Fest**, in his biography of Hitler, declares that 'the prospects for a "March on Berlin" were by no means unfavourable ... as became clear the next morning, public sentiment was clearly on the side of Hitler and the Kampfbund'. What do you think?

The gamble had failed. Hitler had made serious errors of judgement in counting on von Kahr's, and particularly von Lossow's, backing, over-estimating support for the Nazis outside Bavaria, and assuming that the Republic was about to collapse. But at his subsequent trial, he 'unexpectedly ceased to be the accused and became the accuser' (Fest), resulting in the minimum sentence possible. Hitler retired to enjoy his 'university education at the expense of the state', to compose a 'coherent' statement of his beliefs in *Mein Kampf*, which was to become the necessary Bible for the movement, and to rejoice in the fact that the trial had given him access to a national audience to which he could claim that he alone had dared to strike a blow for German nationalism.

It is now possible to see how Hitler might regard the failed putsch as a great piece of good fortune. But more important consequences were to follow. The first was the abandonment of plans to overturn the regime by force and the decision to work within the constitution to gain power by legitimate political means – 'we shall have to hold our noses and enter the Reichstag'. Power must be gained with legality preserved, before the 'revolution from above', in Stalin's phrase, could begin. Secondly, the party must be reorganised, Hitler's leadership regained, possible rivals defeated and a party bureaucracy instituted. On 27 February 1925, after Hitler had spoken for two hours and promised his resignation after a year if his leadership was unsuccessful, the leading contenders shook hands on the platform. Henceforth known as *der Führer*, Hitler was able to direct Gregor Strasser to North Germany and force Ernst Röhm's resignation – thus eliminating his two most serious rivals and establishing his own authoritarian leadership of the party. An efficient administrative apparatus was created at party headquarters, gauleiters and local party organisations were brought under control, the political role of the SA was stressed and the foundations were laid for what Fest describes as a 'shadow state'. By these means Hitler was able to persuade conservatives, nationalists, even the Reichswehr, that he was a reliable ally, whose extremism was only necessary to mobilise the mass support they needed.

Between 1924 and 1928, Hitler succeeded not only in bringing new life to the party after the fiasco in Munich, but also in making it accept his new disguise as 'Adolphe Légalité', which was to bring its reward in the political negotiations that eventually made him Chancellor. It is easy to see the failure of 1923 as the necessary precursor of the triumph ten years later; without it and the consequent change in policy, Hitler's success appears impossible.

Conclusion. The core of this question lies in the final sentence of the conclusion: **was the failure of 1923 the necessary precursor of 1933?** Can you envisage Hitler's eventual triumph as coming without the changes in tactics and in party organisation carried through between 1924 and 1928? And would those changes have been made had there been no failed putsch in 1923? Perhaps the conclusion might have been a little longer in order to stress the answers to these questions.

Mini essay plan

Paragraph 1	Introduction. Means by which the truth of this statement may be tested.
Paragraph 2	The situation in 1923, in Germany and in Bavaria.
Paragraph 3	Events, 8/9 November.
Paragraph 4	Immediate results of this failed coup.
Paragraph 5	Consequences in the longer term, 1924–8.
Paragraph 6	Conclusion. Failure in 1923 the necessary precursor of success in 1933.

General comments

Related questions

1 With reference to the period 1919 to 1928, discuss the view that 'the outcome of the First World War fatally weakened the prospects for the survival of democracy in Germany'.

2 'The Republic grew in strength; the Nazi Party stagnated.' How accurate is this verdict on the years 1924–8?

3 Why was Hitler able to come to power only ten years after the failed Munich putsch of 1923?

Questions on this period can stretch **from 1919 to 1933.** They should be viewed alongside those on the **Weimar Republic** (see **Nazi Germany, Essay 2**). **Questions 1 and 3** are concerned with long periods (**Question 1** is a **concealed relative importance** question) and, particularly in **Question 3**, the planning will be difficult in relation to what to leave out. **Question 2** is a little easier, but the topic is not a particularly good one to choose for revision. Better, perhaps, to concentrate on **'Weimar Republic' questions.**

Exam Success Guide

Essay 2

'The main problem with the Weimar Republic is
not that it eventually collapsed, but that it
survived for so long.' Discuss.

Tackling the question

A not unusual **'not that ... but that ...'**
type of quotation question. The
answer must survey the truth of both
parts: was the collapse of the Weimar
Republic a problem and was its *survival* a
problem? The answer will consider whether
its collapse was inevitable and why it
happened.

Answer

Guidance notes

The eventual collapse of the Weimar Republic after Hitler
became Chancellor in January 1933 is usually put down to 'the
vague collective idea of a "world economic crisis"'. Dr Bracher,
however, sees more importance in 'an understanding of the
structural political problems of the Weimar Republic and the
fatal chinks in it which provided openings for authoritarian and
totalitarian counter movements'. Most students of the period
would agree that the Weimar governments faced two periods of
particular crisis (1919–23 and 1929–33) with a measure of
economic and political stability between (1924–8). Each of these
periods will be examined with a view to discovering those forces
and events which tended towards survival or collapse, before an
attempt is made to view the 14 years of Weimar's life as a
whole.

Introduction. Notice how the
relatively long life of the Weimar
Republic can be divided into **three
distinct periods**, two of crisis and
one of stability. You should
always try to split up a longish
period in this way; in the case of
Weimar rule the divisions are
obvious; in other periods you may
have to impose your own, more
artificial, divisions upon them.
Your planning will now become
much easier.

The Weimar Republic was 'flawed from the moment of its birth
... the product of military defeat and the social distress caused by
the war ... a knee-jerk reaction to crisis, rather than a genuine
desire for fundamental change' (Layton). The old bureaucratic
machinery remained in place, and with added power as ministers
came and went in transitory governments, while the Reichstag

Paragraphs. Although the
quotation which starts this
paragraph is rather long
(however, the last phrase
should be easily memorable), it
does provide an excellent

Essay 2

'topic sentence' which is illustrated by the remainder of the paragraph. A suitable quotation can often do this.

(where sovereignty was supposed to reside) failed in its two vital tasks – the making of policy and of those necessary compromises which should provide the solution for social and political conflicts. Proportional representation might provide theoretically perfect democracy, but it also produced too many irreconcilable parties with too little faith in the system and providing too little hope of stable majority governments. The theory of the 'stab in the back' and the tarnishing of the government by the acceptance of the Versailles treaty provided ample ammunition for parties in opposition. Finally, the army 'was not clearly subordinate to the state' and, under the leadership of von Seeckt, was prepared to do no more than 'tolerate the Republic for the time being in its own interests' (Hiden).

The new Republic survived its first period of crisis (1919–23) largely because of the Reichswehr's attitude. Its leaders put the unity of the army first when the Kapp putsch (1920) threatened Berlin; it was always happy to suppress left-wing insurrections; in 1923, Hitler's abortive putsch was crushed by the Munich police, preventing Seeckt's claim that *Reichswehr does not fire on Reichswehr* from being put to the test. This was the last direct challenge to the state from extremists on the left and right, but important social groups remained opposed to the Republic.

Question. One obvious question at this point concerns the ability of **Stresemann**, had he survived, to bring the Weimar Republic through the slump. Although one can never be sure of the 'might have beens' of history, the subsequent history of Germany does not give one much optimism that its postwar government would have survived its second crisis, whoever might have been its leader. But it's also fair to agree with **William Carr** that 'it is inconceivable that Hitler could ever have come to power had not the Weimar Republic been subjected to the unprecedented strain of a world economic crisis'.

The period covered by Stresemann's holding of the offices of Chancellor and Foreign Minister appeared to offer the best hope of survival for the beleaguered Republic: the stabilisation of the economy with the introduction of the Reichsmark; foreign aid, especially from the United States, under the Dawes Plan (1924) which partially solved the problem of reparations; by 1928, a 120% increase in coal and steel output and 300,000 houses and flats built in a year; health insurance extended to cover twenty million people – all this gave hope for the future. Politically, the German Nationalist parties gave their support to the Republic, with the Communists and the Nazis the only parties remaining hostile. Abroad, Germany was no longer treated as an outcast: Stresemann negotiated the Locarno Treaties (1925), Germany joined the League in 1926, the Young Plan seemed finally to solve the reparations question in 1929 and the last Allied troops left the Rhineland in 1930.

Although William Carr sees Stresemann as 'a statesmanlike figure of immense ability and industry ... a gifted orator and a dynamic and vigorous personality', his successful domination of the government had obscured structural weaknesses in the German economy, notably a chronically depressed agriculture and a dependence on foreign loans which might be withdrawn very rapidly. In October 1927 the boom on the American stock market collapsed and with Stresemann's death in the same month the economic and political situations were simultaneously destabilised. Had economic prosperity lasted longer, the Republic might have gained a greater measure of popularity with the German people: had the depression been shorter and less intense, the Republic might have survived.

Once the slump had begun, the chances of survival were slight. Brüning, like his immediate successors, 'was trying above all to achieve legitimacy and a majority in the Reichstag' (Salmon). The conservative governments of the period were at least trying to preserve Weimar democracy and the concept of a popular mandate for the necessary political decisions. Hitler alone had made no secret of his anti-democratic intentions and it seems clear that these were shared by a considerable part of the German population and important sections of the establishment – 'that very small circle of busy-bodies ... utterly irresponsible extra constitutional exponents of political and economic tendencies and illusions'. Von Schleicher might pull the strings which brought Brüning's appointment and dismissal; von Papen was to oust von Schleicher by similar intrigues when he assumed the Chancellorship himself. Both thought they could 'tame' Hitler and the Nazis, while it was the support of 'bankers, industrialists and agrarians ... the entourage of the ancient President, especially his son' (Carsten) which brought Hitler to power and an end to the Weimar Republic.

What were the causes of Weimar's long survival and eventual collapse? The Reichswehr had played the major, if unwilling, part in the survival of the regime in the first period of crisis (1923); Stresemann's success lasted too short a time to rally public support for the system; the slump which began in 1930 was too long and too severe for that fragile system to survive. Hitler's triumph was not inevitable and was the product of disastrous political manoeuvring, but the Weimar Republic was always unlikely to survive the crisis of 1929.

Conclusion. Here, the reasons already discussed for the long survival and eventual collapse of Weimar are summarised. The fact that Hitler's triumph was not inevitable is stressed, although not actually part of the question; you may feel that more evidence should be given as to why 'the Weimar Republic was always unlikely to survive the crisis of 1929'.

Essay 2

General comments

Related questions

1 'In the 1920s the Weimar Republic was able to resist non-democratic forces; in the 1930s it was not.' Why was this?

2 How stable was the Weimar Republic by 1929?

3 'The Weimar Republic had few firm friends and too many enemies.' How satisfactory do you find this explanation of its collapse?

Questions on the Weimar Republic must be clearly distinguished from those on the triumph of the Nazis. Always remember that the two events are not necessarily linked; the Nazis were by no means certain to fill the vacuum left by the failure of Weimar. All these questions revolve around the causes of Weimar's demise; once you've prepared a reliable list of these, planning of answers to these questions shouldn't be too difficult. **Stephen Lee**, *European Dictatorships*, **pages 145–51**, provides a good start.

Why was Hitler appointed Chancellor in January 1933 after being refused that office in August 1932?

Tackling the question

You could call this a **'why then rather than then?'** type of question, although they are not very common. What is important, though, is the usual concept of **balance**. The two parts of the question (how and why Hitler was refused the Chancellorship in August and how and why he was offered it in January) need balance as far as the amount of detail in each is concerned. You should consider whether the specimen essay has achieved this: particularly whether there's enough detail in the answer to the second question, and whether the paragraph on the people who supported the Nazis is strictly necessary for this answer or might be replaced by more detail on the events between August and January and their causes. Again, how necessary is the detail given for events from May 1928 to July 1932? Don't be afraid to criticise specimen essays!

Answer

Guidance notes

Noakes and Pridham have called the period August–December 1932 'the crisis months' in the Nazis' 'struggle for power'. To understand their importance – and eventual outcome in January 1933 – it is necessary to examine the remarkable rise of Hitler and his party from 1928 until the apparent triumph of the July election of 1932; to determine whence support for the party had come; to analyse the complex negotiations of the last months of 1932 and to note the bitter disappointment of the party which followed electoral victory; and to explain, finally, the reasons for the remarkable change in Hitler's fortunes in January 1933.

The election of May 1928 had resulted in unexpected defeat for the NSDAP – 100,000 fewer votes than in 1924 and only 12 seats. Now the strategy had to change. Hitler called for 'a switch in priorities from the cities to the countryside' (Bullock). In the autumn of 1928, the party assumed its first role in national politics with its campaign against the Young Plan in alliance with

Statistics. The results of elections are particularly important during this period. If possible you should give the number of seats obtained, the percentage of the vote and size of the party in the Reichstag. One of the sets of statistics which it is necessary to learn by heart in this period is that covering the election results of the Nazi Party during its short existence: make out a clear and compact list of these, enclose it in a plastic wallet and carry it around with you until you can use it in answers almost without thinking.

Hugenburg and the DNVP. The Depression was beginning to add to the growing 'crisis of the bourgeois parties' and Hitler saw that this was his chance. Nazi appeals for unity and authority in the state bore fruit in the unnecessary election unwisely called by the new Chancellor, Brüning, in September 1930. The Nazis gained 18.6% of the popular vote, securing 107 seats and becoming the second largest party in the Reichstag.

Hitler's party had made its breakthrough into national politics; now he had to find a way to convert popular support into a National Socialist government led by himself. As Bullock suggests, he could use his popular support to press for inclusion in the government and the threat of SA violence if he was excluded. Hitler played his cards well, leaving all his options open (a Reichstag majority, a coup, authoritarian rule by Article 48) while steadily pursuing his goal (like Stalin, as Bullock notes) and using his remarkable ability to retain the confidence of his often restive supporters with the help of the growing 'Hitler myth', which served as a substitute for a detailed programme. Patience was essential, but Bullock finds four factors of which Hitler could take advantage: the intensification of the Depression; its consequences, including the increased vote for the radical left and right and the increased attacks on the Republic; the Reichswehr's *rapprochement* with the Republic after Hindenburg had become President and their attempt to secure political stability for continued rearmament; finally, the increasing substitution of presidential for parliamentary government. Hitler might fail to gain the presidency in April 1932, but the vote for him in the second ballot reached 13.4 million. The election in July made the NSDAP the largest party in the Reichstag with 13,745,000 votes and 230 seats – in four years the party had gained nearly 13 million votes.

Where had this new support for National Socialism come from? Most historians agree that it was largely from the middle class (the *Mittelstand*) which may be subdivided into the old *Mittelstand* (artisans, small retailers, peasant farmers) and the new (white-collar workers, civil servants, primary school teachers). Many of the former, who became the core of Nazi support, had joined the movement before 1929; the latter 'helped to boost the Nazi vote ... to 13.5 million in 1932' (Lee). Blue-collar workers remained remarkably loyal to the SDP and the KDP because of their membership of the trade unions; the upper classes were sometimes attracted by Hitler's anti-communist

Definitions. You should be quite clear what the phrase **'Hitler myth'** actually means. **Ian Kershaw's** *Hitler Myth* will tell you all you need to know.

stance, but the chief support from the wealthy came after Hitler was appointed Chancellor. 'To some extent the appeal of Nazism transcended class barriers altogether' (Lee): Protestants, women, the young were all attracted by 1932. But in spite of the vast increase in their vote, the Nazis still lacked a majority which could give them the automatic right to power.

During the 'crisis months' which followed, the refusal of Hindenburg and von Papen to offer anything more than the Vice-Chancellorship on 13 August was to put great strain on party loyalties. Somehow Hitler was able to preserve the policy of legality, in the face of its apparent failure, even after the resignation of Gregor Strasser which badly dented party morale. The fighting of yet another election in November, when the NSDAP vote dropped by two million and the KPD vote increased significantly, was a further blow. Well might Goebbels reflect at Christmas that 'this year has brought us everlasting bad luck'.

But the tide was turning. The new Chancellor, Schleicher, had failed to gain the mass support which he had promised Hindenburg, with his policy based on backing from the trade unions and the 'moderate' Nazis under Strasser. Von Papen was determined to bring him down and was now ready to see Hitler as Chancellor. They reached agreement on 4 January, but it took almost another month of tortuous negotiations before Hindenburg's suspicion of the 'Bavarian corporal' could be overcome, Hugenburg's economic conditions satisfied and the Reichswehr's support ensured by the appointment of the pro-Nazi von Blomberg as Minister of Defence.

Question. The obvious questions on this topic concern responsibility for the changes which took place in the fortunes of the Nazi Party over the whole period 1928 to 1933 and particularly in the last months of 1932. Was Hitler ultimately responsible for his party's success, or was it the foolish schemes of von Papen and his allies or the fumbling reactions of the tired and aged Hindenburg that brought Hitler the Chancellorship, which he had held out for with such determination? The specimen essay does not answer this question. Do you think it should do so and what should the answer be?

Such a remarkable reversal of fortune as brought Hitler to the Chancellorship on 30 January 1933 caused Goebbels to confide in his diary that 'it all seems like a fairy story'. But it was in fact the result of 'ambitious and misguided men [who] sought to make history' and were confident, like von Papen, that Hitler would be 'no danger at all'. Nor must Hitler's own contribution be forgotten: the steadfast adherence to the policy of legality, the extraordinary control over the unruly party, the insistence on the Chancellorship, and the selling of the idea that – in the words of a Nazi slogan – 'National Socialism is the opposite of what exists today'.

Mini essay plan

Paragraph 1	Introduction. August to December 1932, 'the crisis months' in the Nazi struggle for power.
Paragraph 2	The election of 1928 to the election of September 1930.
Paragraph 3	Breakthrough into national politics to the election of July 1932.
Paragraph 4	Where the support for the Nazis came from.
Paragraph 5	The 'crisis months' of 1932.
Paragraph 6	The events of January 1933.
Paragraph 7	Conclusion. Hitler's reversal of fortune due to 'ambitious and misguided men' and his own contribution.

General comments

Related questions

1 'It all seems like a fairy story.' Was the Nazi seizure of power an historical accident, as Goebbels confided to his diary, or the inevitable result of 'a host of powerful trends, partly historical in nature, [which] pointed towards what happened on 30 January'.

2 Assess the responsibility of Brüning, Schleicher, von Papen and Hindenburg for the Nazis' rise to power.

3 How important a part did Hitler play in the Nazis' rise to power between 1928 and 1933?

Questions on the Nazi seizure of power tend to require detailed knowledge of the period. If you're happy with this, then it's a possible topic to include in your revision.

Question 1 requires an understanding of the 'powerful trends' which led to 30 January. You should read pages 366–84 in *Hitler* by **Joachim Fest** to help you to answer this one.

Question 2 indicates a clear plan involving a paragraph (or two) on the part played by each of the characters named, and some indication of their relative importance in the final outcome.

Question 3 covers a lot of ground – balance will be therefore be important – and must take into account the alternative reasons for success.

Essay 4

To what extent had Germany undergone a political revolution between January 1933 and August 1934?

Tackling the question

Beware questions including the word 'revolution'! As here, they usually ask 'to what extent ...?' You have to judge whether the changes are sufficiently fast and fundamental to qualify as revolutionary.

Now is a good moment to give you some advice about converting your question analysis into the mini essay plan which will provide you with a good answer to the question. **First**, you may find it helpful to **re-phrase the question in your own words**: 'the question is concerned with the extent to which the political changes between January 1933 and August 1934 amounted to a revolution'.

Secondly, you should decide on your **immediate 'gut-reaction' answer** to the question: 'personal dictatorship had replaced liberal democracy but there were still links with Germany's past which had not

been destroyed, thus only a limited revolution'.

Thirdly, you must decide on **up to six facts which support your answer**. In this case, I've picked out the following: **(1)** Hitler's position as Chancellor in January 1933; **(2)** his first aim, to eliminate the Reichstag; **(3)** now Weimar democracy could be destroyed by revolutions from above and below; **(4)** further calls for a 'second revolution' could be prevented by destroying the power of the SA; **(5)** the death of Hindenburg allowed Hitler to become Führer; **(6) BUT** the influence of the army, the civil service, big business, even the Christian churches remained and prevented the revolution from being complete.

Lastly, this factual evidence must be turned into a mini essay plan. Here, you can see that I've not given (6) a paragraph on its own but have included it in the conclusion. Should I have done this?

Answer

Guidance notes

Historians should never tire of emphasising the true definition of the term 'revolution': 'a fundamental change, an overturning of existing political conditions'. To examine the extent of the changes which took place during this period, and to judge their revolutionary implications, it is important to decide how far comparisons should be made with the years of the Weimar Republic, or with the political traditions which had prevailed since 1871. These changes must be examined in detail – in particular, the decree of 28 February 1933, the Enabling Act and the meaning of the Night of the Long Knives – before the situation when Hitler became Chancellor can be compared with that when he was able to unite the offices of Chancellor and President in the new title of Führer.

When Hitler was appointed Chancellor at the end of January 1933, there was no question of his having achieved absolute power. Only three members of the Cabinet were Nazis, von Papen was Vice-President, the Nazis had no majority in the Reichstag and the Chancellor could be dismissed by the President at any time. It seemed that von Papen was right to boast: 'Don't worry, we've hired him.' The Conservatives could make policy 'which Hitler would "sell" to the country through his party and propaganda machine' (Noakes and Pridham). But Hitler had a number of important advantages. He led the largest political party in Germany; Goebbels now had access to the facilities of the state for his propaganda machine; Goering and Frick had considerable control over the police; while von Papen's removal of the Prussian government in July 1932 had seriously weakened opposition in the states to further centralisation. Hitler could play the card of national unity in his 'Appeal to the German People' (31 January 1933) and speak of a 'national uprising' to overcome 14 years of demoralisation.

Factual evidence. A lot of explanation has been left out in this paragraph: should some have been given of the results of the election of March 1933, of the Civil Service Act and of the Enabling Act? Perhaps you could expect the reader to know the terms of the Enabling Act; some explanation of how the Civil Service Act 'controlled' the revolution from below seems necessary.

Hitler aimed first to 'eliminate the Reichstag as an effective organ'. In spite of the opportunities provided by Goering's manipulation of the Prussian police, the Reichstag fire and the resulting decree of 28 February (for Mommsen, a kind of coup d'état) which suspended most civil liberties and strengthened the power of the central government over the states, the Nazis did not win the decisive majority they wanted, being still dependent on their alliance with the Nationalist Party. The ensuing 'revolution from below' had to be controlled by the 'Law for the Re-establishment of the Professional Civil Service' (7 April 1933), and the impressive propaganda spectacle of the 'Day of Potsdam' set the scene for the passing of the Enabling Act, of doubtful constitutionality but great propaganda value, removing the doubts of the judiciary and the civil service about subsequent Nazi actions and becoming the 'constitutional foundation-stone of the Third Reich' (Layton).

Now *Gleichschaltung* ('co-ordination') could begin with the object of destroying Weimar democracy and substituting one-party dictatorship. A combined revolution from above and below was aimed at destroying German federalism, the trade unions and all other political parties. Laws of 31 March and 7 April ensured the party a majority in all state assemblies and appointed special Reich Governors for the states. On 2 May, all German workers' organisations were merged into DAF (the German Labour Front) and the power of the union movement was broken. The Communist Party had been proscribed after the Reichstag fire, the Social Democrats were banned on 22 June and all other parties had dissolved themselves when the decree of 14 July proclaimed the Nazi Party as the only legal party in the Reich. But, by mid-1933 no impression had been made on the conservative bastions of the army, the Christian churches and big business. Hitler was determined to control the 'revolution from below' to avoid antagonising his support among conservatives.

On 6 July, Hitler declared an end to revolution, whose 'full spate' must now 'be guided into the secure bed of evolution'. But calls for a 'second revolution' continued, particularly from the populist, anti-capitalist SA who felt that, having won the battle of the streets, they had tasted few of the fruits of victory. But Röhm's call for a genuine 'National Socialist revolution' was less menacing than his plans for a 'People's Militia' which the Reichswehr would never accept. Although Hitler charac-teristically hesitated before acting against the SA, there was no doubt that he would eventually do so – the army played too important a role in his dreams of foreign expansion. Hindenburg's approaching death triggered the Night of the Long Knives; the threat from the SA was effectively countered and the conservatives would not now prevent Hitler from combining the offices of Chancellor and President in his new role as Führer, with the armed forces swearing loyalty to him rather than to the state.

At the Nuremberg rally, September 1934, Hitler could now proclaim with more certainty that 'people could not live on revolutions'. How fundamental had been the changes he had brought about in a bare eighteen months? At first sight, it seems clear that the liberal democracy of Weimar had been replaced by the mirror image of personal dictatorship. If the comparison is taken further back in German history, the destruction of German federalism, of any political opposition and of the power of the Reichstag can be seen as equally foreign to the political traditions of the *Kaiserreich*. But there were also important continuities with that era, represented by the continued existence and

Conclusion. The more one looks at this essay, the more it seems that at least a paragraph should be given to the evidence for the limited nature of the revolution and to include reference to it only in the conclusion is not sufficient. The fact that the conclusion is partly centred on this point of limited revolution is a strong argument for giving it more prominence – and a paragraph of its own is the most obvious way of doing this. You see, I told you to approach these answers in a sceptical mood!

independent influence of the army, the civil service, big business and even the Christian churches. 'Hitler's willingness to enter into political partnership with these representatives of the old Germany' meant that his 'national revolution' 'was strictly limited in scope; it involved political compromise, and it refrained from fundamental social and economic change' (Layton).

Paragraph 1	Introduction. Correct comparisons important in gauging revolutionary changes.
Paragraph 2	Hitler's position as Chancellor in January 1933: apparent weakness and actual strength.
Paragraph 3	Hitler's first aim: to eliminate the Reichstag. Events up to the Enabling Act.
Paragraph 4	*Gleichschaltung* – events to mid-1933.
Paragraph 5	Events: 6 July–2 August 1934.
Paragraph 6	Conclusion. Weimar liberal democracy had been replaced by personal dictatorship, but there were also continuities with an older Germany, which meant that the revolution was strictly limited in scope.

Mini essay plan

General comments

Related questions

1 How and why were the Nazis able to tighten their grip on power so easily between 1933 and 1934?

2 'A turning-point in the history of the Third Reich.' Consider this assessment of the purge of the SA leadership of 30 June 1934.

3 Assess the importance of the Enabling Act, *Gleichschaltung* and the 'Night of the Long Knives' in establishing the Nazi dictatorship.

Question 1 demands an understanding of the reasons for the lack of opposition to the Nazis during 1933 and 1934. In **Question 2** you must know enough about the causes, events and results of 30 June 1934 to answer a complete question on that topic. **Question 3** also requires knowledge of the Enabling Act and *Gleichschaltung*: all three are vital for answers on this topic, which is a good one to add to your revision list as the questions are normally straightforward.

Essay 5

How far do you see Hitler as a 'weak dictator' in his command of domestic policy in the Third Reich?

Tackling the question

'**How far...?**' questions are always coming up. First note what the answer to **Question 11** in the introduction to this book says about them, particularly the various phrases which introduce them. How many questions can you find in this book of this type? Remember that the following questions, although the wording is different, are of this type: **Communist Russia 4, 5, 8, 10, 11; Fascist Italy 2; Nazi Germany 1, 4**. If you're in doubt, try to rephrase the question using 'how far?' to introduce it.

The other important thing to remember about these questions is that the answer requires you to discuss and balance arguments for and against the proposition. Here this involves examining the case for Hitler as a 'weak dictator' and the opposite argument that he was 'master of the Third Reich'. The cases made by **'Intentionalists'** and **'Structuralists'** (it's a pity the names are not more self-explanatory; you must be quite sure of their meaning before you use the terms) must also play a part in your argument.

Answer

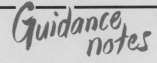

Guidance notes

Hans Mommsen described a Hitler 'unwilling to take decisions, frequently uncertain, exclusively concerned with upholding his prestige and personal authority, influenced in the strongest fashion by his current entourage, in some respects a weak dictator'. The other side in the great postwar debate may be represented by the famous comment of Norman Rich that 'the point cannot be stressed too strongly: Hitler was master in the Third Reich'. Entwined with this problem is the further one, as Kershaw stresses, of those 'Intentionalists' ('deducing the development of the Third Reich from Hitler's ideological intentions') and the 'Structuralists' ('seeking to locate [Hitler's] importance within the framework of numerous additional pressures built into the governmental system ... considering the Führer ... in his functional role within a multi-dimensional (polycratic) system of rule'). To find the answer to these questions, one must examine the relationship between party and state in the Third Reich, assess the continuing influence of old power-blocs represented by the army, the civil service and big business, compared with the new apparatus of the police state, and finally attempt an analysis of the role of the Führer himself.

Evidence. These examples of three different explanations of the administrative chaos of the Third Reich are particularly useful as they illustrate clearly three different approaches to the same problem.

The Weimar constitution, never formally abolished, was not replaced by a 'Hitler constitution'. Historians are largely agreed on the administrative chaos of Nazi rule: Mommsen would claim that Hitler failed to control it; the 'Intentionalists' would find a deliberate policy of 'divide and rule'; while the 'Structuralists' would point to 'a multi-dimensional power-structure, in which Hitler's own authority was only an element (if a very important one)'. Hitler never made clear, perhaps wisely, what he believed the true nature of the party–state relationship to be. The Nazi leadership might be anxious to 'establish Nazi control over the State ... [but] ... could not afford to allow the bureaucratic machine to be damaged through disruption by unqualified party elements' (Noakes and Pridham). All former ministries were retained; the civil service continued to function; many party members were disappointed at the continuity which seemed to be the hallmark of the 'Nazi revolution' they had hoped to bring about. Instead, Hitler developed a system of parallel institutions, often competing with each other. Special Deputies, such as the General Inspector of German Roads and the Youth Leader of the Reich, overlapped and conflicted with the Ministries of Transport and Education. New offices, such as that of Deputy Führer, had powers over regular ministries. In local government, traditional Minister-Presidents clashed and competed with newly-appointed Reich Governors. Thus the party's main task, after controlling and educating the masses, was to supervise rather than run the state. Eventually, and most important of all, there emerged an autonomous SS-Gestapo-SD complex which could claim to embody the real Nazi revolution by creating 'an organisation which "potentially superseded the state" and perhaps the party as well' (Williamson).

Factual evidence. Be particularly careful to write 'Hitler developed ...' only when you have actual evidence of Hitler's personal involvement in the development.

The Reichswehr, which had played a considerable role in the political system since 1871, appeared in a strong position after Hitler's defeat of its rival, the SA, in June 1934. Collaboration continued as Hitler pressed ahead with rearmament and introduced conscription (March 1935). But the power of the SS was growing and Hitler was becoming impatient with the conservatism of the High Command. When Blomberg and Fritsch voiced their doubts over the feasibility of Hitler's plans set out at the Hossbach meeting, they were forced out of office on trumped-up charges; the position of War Minister was abolished and Hitler became Commander-in-Chief of the armed forces with his own high command. After 1938, the army's political power was much reduced; the outbreak of war made opposition both unpatriotic and treasonable, while the failure of the Bomb Plot brought final subordination to the party and the SS. Like the army, the civil service continued to function in support of the regime, governed by patriotism and its legalistic training, which enabled it 'to rationalise almost any action, however immoral, provided it took the form of a law or decree' (Noakes and Pridham). Finally, Hitler had no wish to restructure the economy, providing it produced the results he wanted: 'economic recovery and the elimination of unemployment in the short run, German rearmament in the longer run' (Bullock). He might use, as Noakes and Pridham describe, 'a combination of the carrot and the stick' towards big business, he might subject it to controls, but it remained in private hands and many of its leaders enjoyed great profit from rearmament.

There is general agreement on the enormous influence of the SS-Gestapo-SD complex: it 'made foreign, military and agricultural policy ... administered occupied territories ... and maintained itself economically with autonomous enterprises' (Lee). As a power-bloc, it eventually outstripped all others – it was the 'key interest group in the Third Reich'.

The roots of Hitler's style of leadership may be found in his personality, his pre-1933 experience as party leader and his permanent claim to charismatic leadership. He hated paper-work, preferred to avoid decisions and only in the last resort became the 'remote umpire handing down decisions from on high' (Petersen). As charismatic leader, Hitler could always go outside the party hierarchy before 1933; after 1 August 1934, this charismatic leadership was 'transferred from the party to the German state and nation to form the basis of the Nazi regime' (Noakes and Pridham).

Question. In this particular question, the focus is very much on the part Hitler personally played in the direction of domestic policy, thus the warning given on p. 100 is particularly apt. In the chaotic conditions of Nazi rule and given Hitler's well-known aversion to decision making, it is always going to be hard to establish who was actually in charge. Be ready to acknowledge that answers to this type of question must be tentative.

It is hard to see Hitler as a 'weak dictator' in domestic affairs when the course of events, at least until 1943, followed so closely his 'intentions'. But the omnipotence implied in the title 'master of the Third Reich' is equally misleading and Kershaw is surely right in stressing 'the need to look for a synthesis of "intention" and "structure", rather than see them as polarised opposites'.

Essay 5

Mini essay plan

Paragraph 1   Introduction. 'Weak dictator' versus 'master of the Third Reich' and 'Intentionalists' versus 'Structuralists'.

Paragraph 2   The relationship between party and state in the Third Reich.

Paragraph 3   The influence of the old power-blocs: army, civil service and big business.

Paragraph 4   The influence of the new SS-Gestapo-SD complex.

Paragraph 5   The role of the Führer.

Paragraph 6   Conclusion. Neither description wholly true – need for synthesis.

General comments

Related questions

1 How valid is the term 'totalitarian' as a description of the Third Reich?

2 Why and with what justification have some historians cast doubts upon the extent of Hitler's power in Germany between 1933 and 1939?

3 To what extent would you agree with the description of the Third Reich as the 'SS state'?

It's hardly surprising to find the same question on **'totalitarianism'** being asked about the Nazi state as about the Italian fascist one. You could refer to **Kershaw**, *The Nazi Dictatorship*, **Chapter 2**, for help here. Helpful and rather easier to follow are **de Grand**, *Fascist Italy and Nazi Germany*, **Chapter 5**; **Layton**, *The Third Reich*, **Chapter 5**; and **Williamson**, *The Third Reich*, **Chapter 6**.

Question 2 could be answered using much of the same material as is in the specimen essay; you should try adapting its **MEP** to the new question.

Question 3 obviously needs much more detail on the '**SS state**' than is available in the (too?) brief paragraph in the specimen essay. Look for details in **Noakes and Pridham**, *Nazism 1919–1945*, **Volume 2, Chapter 22; Bracher**, *The German Dictatorship*, **pages 435–50 and 506–20**.

Whether you choose this as a revision topic may well depend on how much new material you need to digest.

Essay 6

Did Nazism produce a social revolution in Germany during the period of the Third Reich?

Tackling the question

Here we go again – another **'revolution question'**! This time it's a social revolution, even more difficult to recognise than a political one. In this case, the arguments focus particularly on **Schoenbaum's two types of reality**; it's most important that you understand the difference between them (see **Layton**, *The Third Reich*, **pages 109–13** for a simplified but clear account).

Let's practise the drill for changing question analysis into MEP. The **'gut-reaction'** answer to the question of whether Nazism produced a social revolution in Germany could be that the Nazis produced no social revolution, either in the minds of the people or in their social classes or institutions. A defining paragraph on *Volksgemeinschaft* is obviously necessary; further paragraphs on change and continuity in class structure, the place of women and the family, youth policy, religious allegiances and success in implanting racial theories should provide sufficient evidence for a reasoned conclusion. In order to stay within the **six-paragraph limit**, there must be some combination of topics within paragraphs. This will produce the **MEP** which follows this answer.

Answer

Guidance notes

'To use the term revolution is to enter a semantic minefield' (Jeremy Noakes). To explore the concept of a social revolution is even more dangerous. The question of how far the Nazis were able to produce a social revolution during the Third Reich has divided historians since 1945. Professor Kershaw sees three main categories of interpretation: the first, appealing particularly to Marxist historians, finds that 'the fundamental *substance* of society remained unchanged'; in contrast, 'liberal' scholars see profound changes amounting to a 'social revolution'; a third position dismisses the concept of 'social revolution' because the social effects of Nazi rule were 'contradictory – some "modernising", others reactionary' – although other writers would add that Nazism was 'truly "a revolution of destruction" – of itself and of others on an unparalleled scale'. To test the truth of these different views, it is important to consider Schoenbaum's

Introduction. The third sentence of this introduction illustrates clearly an important fault in writing exam answers – I said you must be critical of them! These **'three categories of interpretation'** might have been helpful in another **MEP** to answer this question; in fact they play no useful part in the plan that I've chosen and aren't referred to again. The introduction would be much better without them.

'interpreted social reality' (the idea of the Volksgemeinschaft and whether it produced any fundamental change in social values) together with the often contradictory changes of 'objective social reality' (modification of class structure, demographic changes affecting women and the family, the efficacy of educational reforms and the effect of the Hitler Youth, continued support for the Christian churches and the effects on the population of the racial prejudices of the regime and its leader).

The Nazis saw their seizure of power as 'the start of a revolution which would transform German society in accordance with their ideology ... a National Social revival that proclaimed it could integrate disparate elements under the banner of a national re-birth for Germany' (Welch). The concept of *Volksgemeinschaft* (people's community) owed something to 'the spirit of 1914', but this *Burgfrieden* could not survive a long war or the dangerous world of Weimar in the 1920s. Aimed particularly at the working class, the subject of oppressive propaganda, strengthened by programmes such as *Winterhilfe* (to help victims of mass unemployment) and the *Eintopf* meal (by which money saved on monthly, one-dish Sunday lunches would go to the needy), *Volksgemeinschaft* has been described as a failure in terms of destroying class differences and religious and family loyalties, although it may have helped to ensure stability for the regime and have been viewed by many 'as an acceptable insurance policy against the alternative, Marxist-Leninism' (Welch).

German class structure underwent no revolution between 1933 and 1945. The old élites were able to absorb the new 'technocrats of power' from the party without losing their identity. Any major changes in the social position of the *Mittelstand* took place only in the chaos of the final phase of the war ('continuity rather than dramatic change was the hallmark down to the mid-war period'); the working class also enjoyed continuity and any changes which had taken place by 1945 were, therefore, 'a product of Nazism's collapse more than of its policies while in power' (Kershaw).

The Nazi view of the role of women was summed up in the slogan: *'Kinde, Kuche, Kirche'*. But the period 1900–33 had seen two important trends: a falling birth-rate (20.3 per thousand in the 1920s to 14.7 per thousand in 1933) and the expansion of female employment by at least a third. Thus the contradiction between Nazi theory and military and economic pressures for a

Definitions. Is it necessary to translate *'Kinde, Kuche, Kirche'*? This seems to me to be a good example of a phrase which you could expect the reader to know and which does not need translation. But make sure that anything you say about it does not raise doubts in the reader's mind about your understanding of what is meant.

larger population and workforce was always present, particularly in wartime. The birth-rate did increase up to 1939, but it is difficult to say how far Nazi population policy was responsible. Wilke claims that the Nazi regime brought 'tremendous changes to the lives of women in the village [of Korle]' – entrance to public life, travel, the crossing of social class boundaries – but most of the changes he describes are more a result of the war than of Nazi policy. Continuity still outweighs changes, which were those typical of an advanced capitalist economy.

Nazi ideology might be expected to have its greatest effect on the youth of Germany with its dynamic ideas of a new and more open society. But even here there was only partial success: Hitler thought 20 years would be needed to produce a true Nazi élite; the changes in the education system seem to have caused a fall in academic standards; the Hitler Youth programme suffered from over-rapid expansion and growing alienation, particularly in wartime, from such hostile rivals as the 'Edelweiss Pirates' and the 'Swing' movement.

The relationship between the Nazi state and the Christian churches was at first conciliatory (exemplified by the concordat with the Papacy in 1933) but later developed into a 'war of attrition' with greater persecution in wartime. However, 'the decline in Church membership was trivial during the 1930s, while religious observance and attendance at services increased sharply during the war years ... everything points to the conclusion that Nazi policy failed categorically to break down religious allegiances' (Kershaw). Moreover, the racial theories which were the core of Nazi ideology had only limited acceptance – in the SS and some sections of the Wehrmacht; existing anti-Semitism was enhanced but, as Kershaw notes, the extreme secrecy surrounding plans for the Final Solution 'is indirect testimony that exposure to Nazi race values had come nowhere near completely eradicating conventional moral standards'.

In conclusion, it is clear that Nazi rule produced no 'social revolution' either in 'objective' or 'interpreted' social reality. Schoenbaum's claim that the idea of the *Volksgemeinschaft* – 'a society that was New Deal and good old days at the same time' – was the reality of the Third Reich in the minds of its citizens is hard to accept; it is much easier to agree that changes in the chief social classes and institutions were no more than those typical of a developing industrial society and that the true 'revolution in German society took place in the wake of the Third Reich' (Layton).

Mini essay plan

Paragraph 1	Introduction. Three main interpretations of what took place in the Third Reich.
Paragraph 2	The concept of *Volksgemeinschaft*.
Paragraph 3	Lack of change in the German class structure, 1933–45.
Paragraph 4	Change and continuity in the place of women and the family.
Paragraph 5	Only partial success in youth policy.
Paragraph 6	Failure to break down religious allegiances and to implant racial theories.
Paragraph 7	Conclusion. No social revolution in German minds or institutions. The revolution came after 1945.

General comments

Related questions

1 How urgently, and with what results, did the Nazi regime attempt to fulfil its promises of a social revolution in Germany?

2 Examine the impact of the Third Reich on German cultural life.

3 'The concept of the *Volksgemeinschaft* was little more than an effective propaganda ploy.' What, in your view, were the real social aims of Nazis in the Third Reich?

The whole question of the social aims of the Nazis and their success or failure presents peculiar difficulties. Problems of definition have already been noted and reliable evidence for and against any sort of social revolution is particularly difficult to find. Questions on this topic are either of a general nature **(Questions 1 and 3)** or more specifically concerned with the impact of the Nazi state on particular aspects of German life, such as German culture **(Question 2)**, religion, youth and the status of women.

Question 1 could be answered with most of the evidence used in the specimen essay, together with some consideration of the urgency of their implementation. **Question 2** requires consideration of various topics under the general heading of **'culture'**. **Question 3** needs a full consideration of the concept of *Volksgemeinschaft* together with an analysis of the 'social aims of the Nazis' (see the chapter 'The Nazi State Reconsidered' by **Michael Geyer**, in **Richard Bessel's** *Life in the Third Reich*).

Altogether, this would **not** be a recommended revision topic.

Essay 7

How successful was the Nazi regime in making the German economy ready for war and what was the social impact of these policies?

Tackling the question

A double question on economics. The first part appears to require the longer answer; I've used only one paragraph to answer the second part. Do you think that this is enough? Remember that when you're considering the question of balance in a double question, the two parts will seldom be equally balanced. Here, the balance is very unequal, but you may think that a single longish paragraph is enough to answer the second question, whereas the first is going to require several paragraphs.

Answer

Guidance notes

'Believe me, the decisive factor is not the theory but the performance of the economy', as Hitler told workers at his Berchtesgaden estate. Hitler's economic views were essentially pragmatic: if the existing economic order could achieve his objectives – economic recovery and rearmament – those in the party who expected an economic revolution would be disappointed. To discover the success or failure of these objectives, it is necessary to examine the changes in Nazi economic policy during the years 1933–9 and to compare them with the policies followed in wartime, before considering their impact on various classes of the German population.

The prewar Nazi economy falls naturally into two phases: that dominated by the President of the Reichsbank and later Economics Minister, Hjalmar Schacht, and the later stage under Goering and the Four-Year Plan (1937–9). When he became Chancellor in 1933, Hitler was unencumbered by economic theory and interested only in autarky (for survival in a future war and to make Germany into a major economic power), deficit financing (to bring down unemployment and to stimulate the economy) and the creation of a *Wehrwirtschaft* (defence economy) which would ensure that Germany, prepared in peacetime for the demands of total war, would not suffer a repetition of the economic collapse of 1918. Such objectives raised questions of 'guns or butter' which were often to dominate Nazi economic planning, particularly at the start when increased popularity for the regime was a political necessity. Schacht, with his international reputation as a financier, was able to persuade big business to become an influential partner with the government, although never to the extent that it was dominated by monopoly capitalism as Marxist historians have claimed. He achieved startling reductions in unemployment, which declined to 1.7 million by 1935; negotiated a series of bilateral trade agreements with Balkan and South American states to acquire essential raw materials; saw industrial production increased by 49.5% between 1933 and 1937. But he was unable to solve recurring balance of payments problems and when he suggested a cut in the rearmament programme as a way out of the crisis reached in 1936, his influence was sure to decline.

Goering and his Four-Year Plan were to replace him. Hitler's 1936 memorandum called for the German economy to be fit for war within four years and the plan thus 'highlighted four priorities: an increase in agricultural production, the retraining of key sectors of the labour force, government regulation of imports and exports, and, above all, the achievement of self-sufficiency in raw materials, such as oil, rubber and metals – if necessary by the development of synthetic substitutes' (Layton). This was certainly an economic turning point and brought much tighter controls over industry by the Nazi state. Its success was mixed. The production of synthetic oil and rubber was well below the targets set, although the production of aluminium and explosives was greatly expanded. Autarky had not been achieved, but 'Germany's reliance on imports had not been exacerbated further, despite the economic growth ... German industrial production had increased by 105% since 1935' (Layton).

However, Germany did not, by 1939, possess a war economy. Klein has argued that this 'partial mobilisation' was a deliberate policy allied to that of *Blitzkrieg* and short wars, providing some butter as well as guns and producing by 1939 a 'scale of Germany's mobilisation for war [which] was quite modest'. This interpretation has been questioned: Overy, for instance, has argued that Hitler always envisaged a long war, but one that would not start until 1943, when his preparations would be complete. Certainly, Britain's economic mobilisation was much quicker between 1939 and 1941; the Soviet Union, too, was eventually able to mobilise her economy fully and effectively.

During the latter half of the war, first Todt and then Speer, with the Central Planning Board, were able to produce a more rapid increase in armaments in spite of Allied bombing. But Germany was still 'massively outproduced by the two peripheral industrial giants – the Soviet Union and the United States' (Lee), with this becoming a major factor in Germany's eventual defeat.

What was the social impact of rearmament between 1933 and 1939? By 1939, Germany had recovered from the Depression: national income was 20% higher in 1938 than ten years before, wages were also higher, unemployment was greatly reduced and it seemed that the German people had received a good deal of butter with their guns. But different classes were affected very differently. The industrial working class had gained regular work, stable rents and some 'strength through joy' in the KDF. But bargaining rights were lost, real wages did not rise above 1929 levels until 1938, and weekly hours worked had risen by 15.2% above 1932 levels. The small landowner suffered from attempts 'to freeze the peasantry into an unchanging class': the Reich Entailed Farm Law (1933) was resented as it forbade the division of farms and restricted their modernisation; the Reich Food Estate 'controlled every aspect of agricultural production and consumption'. Agricultural workers remained poor and migrated to the towns at the rate of 2.5% per annum, while only the wealthy landlords gained from increased land values. Small businessmen made some initial gains, but big business was the NSDAP's main target and it was those firms concerned with rearmament which benefited most (I.G. Farben's profits rising 150% between 1938 and 1942).

Paragraphs. This paragraph will have to be planned on the basis of the impact of rearmament on different classes. Do you think that enough weight has been given to each class? There certainly could be more detail on the effect on big business; this might be at the expense of shortening the preceding paragraph on the economy in wartime which is strictly outside the question, although it requires some coverage.

The effect of the changes in economic policy before 1939 thus tended to benefit the rich rather than the poor or most of the *Mittelstand*; rearmament was only partially successful in providing the means for short wars but not, before 1942, for global war. By then it was too late to save Germany from defeat.

Conclusion. A short conclusion, summing up the answer to both parts of the question.

Introduction. Hitler's economic policy essentially pragmatic. An economic order which could produce his objectives would remain in place.

Some success in Schacht's period (1933–6).

Goering and the Four-Year Plan. Four priorities.

No war economy by 1939. Total mobilisation only in 1941–2.

Paragraph 1

Paragraph 2

Paragraph 3

Paragraph 4

Mini essay plan

Essay 7

Paragraph 5

Paragraph 6

The social impact of rearmament. The effects on various classes.

Conclusion. Rearmament only partially successful by 1939. Effects more beneficial for the rich than the poor, or most of the middle class.

General Comments

Related questions

1 How important was rearmament in promoting the recovery of the German economy between 1933 and 1939?

2 By what methods, and with what success, did the Nazi regime attempt to make the German economy ready to meet the demands of war?

3 Examine the proposition that 'the so-called Nazi economic miracle led directly to a major economic crisis from which the only way out was war'.

We can now take our examination of the **related questions** a step further by discovering exactly how the paragraphs in the specimen essay can be used in the writing of other answers on the same topic. First, though, we must analyse them.

Question 1 is a **'how far …?'** question (remember that such questions are also relative importance questions). The question therefore implies that there were other causes of the recovery of the German economy in this period. What were they?

Question 2 is a **double question ('how … and with what success …?')** with the first part very similar to the first part of the specimen essay.

Question 3, as a **long question** normally does, provides you with the basic plan for an answer: Nazi economic miracle leading to economic crisis leading inevitably to war.

How can the specimen essay help us to answer these questions? **Question 2** could be answered by removing the final paragraph on social impact and substituting another in which the question of 'success' is discussed. In **Question 1** the 'recovery' is covered in **paragraphs 2 and 3** of the specimen essay, although there needs to be a more detailed examination of how far this recovery had got by 1939. At least one more paragraph must examine the importance of rearmament as a cause of this recovery, while another must deal with other, rival causes. In **Question 3, paragraphs 2 and 3** cover the 'economic miracle' and the consequent economic crisis, solved by the Four-Year Plan. More detail on both may be required; certainly there will be a need for one or two further paragraphs discussing the arguments for and against the theory that war was the only way out (see **Lee**, *The European Dictatorships*, pages 175–8 for a discussion of this problem).

Thus the specimen essay provides a good deal of evidence to answer all three questions; the fact that not much extra is required makes this an obvious possibility as a **revision topic**.

Essay 8

Essay 8

In Germany, the concept of 'heroic leadership' was born deep in the 19th century; by 1914 it was seen as part of the expansionist ideology of the time and as a unifying influence in an authoritarian state challenged by the forces of democracy and socialism. It made an obvious appeal to Hitler, but it seems that his progress from 'drummer', preparing the way for the leader, to assuming the call to leadership himself, came after the failed putsch of 1923 and was subsequently made clear in the pages of *Mein Kampf*. When the NSDAP was refounded after Hitler's emergence from prison, the growing 'Führer myth' was seen as compensating for the absence of ideological unity in the movement and, with Goebbels' help, was soon to appeal to all those who longed for a dictator to sweep away the impotent politics of Weimar. After the extraordinary results of the 1930 election 'the NSDAP and its leader were big news – the media talking-point'. As the party grew in strength, the Hitler cult became 'the fulcrum of the Nazi propaganda appeal', the NSDAP was commonly referred to as 'the Hitler movement', while the further title of 'People's Chancellor' was given to the leader. By the beginning of 1933, 'more than thirteen million Germans were at least potential "Hitler believers"'(Kershaw).

The task of turning the potential minority of believers into an actual majority was given to Goebbels when he was appointed minister for National Enlightenment and Propaganda (March 1933). He announced that 'the government intends no longer to leave the people to their own devices' and that his new ministry intended 'to establish political coordination between people and government'. Kershaw notes three general factors which led to the eventual acceptance of the Führer cult by a majority of Germans: firstly, 'the widespread feeling that the Weimar political system and leadership were utterly bankrupt'; secondly, the way in which the underestimated rabble-rouser began to solve the country's many problems; thirdly, the existence of a general ideological consensus among most of the population who favoured anti-Marxism, hostility towards the democratic system with a desire for strong leadership, and a widespread feeling 'that Germany had been badly wronged at Versailles and was threatened by enemies on all sides'. The dynamism of the new government, the pseudo-democracy in the title of 'People's Chancellor', the popular drive against the left after the Reichstag fire, the brilliant stage management of the opening of the Reichstag at the Potsdam Garrison Church together with the later splendour of the Nuremberg rallies, the merging of the offices of Chancellor and President after Hindenburg's death, even, strangely, the 'Night of the Long Knives' – all added to the

Punctuation. A long list, separated by commas, and summarised by a phrase introduced by a **dash** at the end.

'Führer myth'. By 1936, that myth had been firmly established and only needed the additional image of the Führer as a statesman who could win international battles without endangering peace, while in the early years of the war, the title of military genius could be added as the Wehrmacht stormed across Europe with the minimum of casualties.

Only ten days after his appointment as minister, Goebbels was claiming that 'mobilisation of the mind is as necessary as, perhaps even more necessary than, the material mobilisation of the nation'. He and Hitler saw how it might be done: by propaganda which was popular, aimed at the most limited member of the audience, while confining itself to a few points which could be used as slogans; by the spoken word, which introduced mass hysteria more easily than anything written and raised the need for 'the development of a special style of mass meetings' (Bracher). Goebbels saw clearly the importance of radio (by 1939 70% of German homes had a set and there was community radio in factories, offices and cafés) and films, which were to be largely escapist rather than propaganda vehicles (the propaganda element being confined to documentaries, news-reels and party-produced 'shorts'). The press was gradually brought under state control (the 'Editors' Law' of October 1933 being the main weapon) while Goebbels' rival, Max Amann, secured similar control over publishing. All news came from the state-owned press agency (DNB) while the content of newspapers was controlled by directions issued at daily press conferences; wider cultural control came through the Reich Chamber of Culture. This vast machine provided everything necessary for the promulgation of the 'Hitler myth'.

Quotations. This quotation might have been better put into your own words: e.g. 'Goebbels claimed that mobilisation of the mind is probably more necessary than material mobilisation of the nation'. If you're noting a quotation of suitable length for inclusion in an essay, always check whether it could be better expressed in indirect speech.

How successful was Goebbels in spreading the 'Hitler myth'? Although he failed to make the mass of the German people believe in National Socialism, although he could not prevent the Nazi Party from being far less popular than its leader, nevertheless it seems that by 1939 he had achieved a high degree of success in the massive effort to win the hearts and minds of the people for the Führer. But as Hitler came to believe more and more in his own myth, so his judgement was clouded by faith in his own infallibility, and Goebbels' greatest achievement was unable to save the Third Reich and its leader from eventual destruction.

Mini essay plan

Paragraph 1	Introduction. The importance of propaganda in the Third Reich. The 'Hitler myth' as a 'masterly achievement of image building'.
Paragraph 2	The concept of 'heroic leadership' in Germany as a basis for the construction of the 'Hitler myth' before 1933.
Paragraph 3	The post-1933 development of the myth through Goebbels' Ministry of Propaganda.
Paragraph 4	The propaganda machine provides everything necessary for the promulgation of the myth.
Paragraph 5	Conclusion. Goebbels fails to make National Socialism or the Nazi Party popular, but the success of the 'Hitler myth' is undoubtedly his greatest achievement, although it helped to bring about the fall of the Third Reich as Hitler came to believe in it himself.

General comments

Related questions

1 Why did Hitler's popularity grow between 1933 and 1939 while that of his party declined?

2 'The new Ministry [of Popular Enlightenment and Propaganda] has no other aim than to unite the people behind the ideal of the national revolution' (Joseph Goebbels). What methods were employed by Goebbels to achieve this aim and with what success?

3 'Without ... sound films and radio, no victory of National Socialism' (Adolf Hitler). Analyse the methods and effectiveness of the Nazi propaganda machine after 1933 in the light of this statement.

How can the specimen essay help in answering these questions? It can't offer much direct help with **Question 1**, although the growth of Hitler's popularity is obviously dependent on the growth of the 'Hitler myth', which is well covered. One or two paragraphs will, however, be required to cover the decline in the popularity of the party.

In **Question 2**, it will be necessary to show how the propaganda effort succeeded in popularising the 'Hitler myth' but failed in its attempts to 'unite the people behind the ideal of the national revolution'. Again, the failure to make the party as popular as its leader must be supplemented by some explanation of the failure to convert many to the Nazi ideology.

Question 3 is briefly covered in **paragraph 4** of the specimen essay, but much more detail is required on the use of radio and film, with some comparison with other methods.

Although the specimen essay doesn't offer much direct help with these questions, little further work is required to provide a **revision topic** which will cover most possible questions.

Essay 9

'Widespread and totally ineffective.' Discuss this view of popular resistance in the Third Reich.

Tackling the question

Some historical questions have produced very different answers from historians because of their continuing importance. For Germans in the postwar period, questions concerning resistance, or its absence, and the classes or groups which did resist were of particular importance. The division of West and East Germany and their different and antagonistic ideologies increased that importance.

In West Germany, resistance was seen as 'essentially bourgeois, Christian, and individual' **(Kershaw)**, while in the GDR 'the near-exclusive emphasis ... upon the heroic underground resistance of the KPD [the German Communist Party] meant the deliberate down-playing of all other forms of opposition' **(Kershaw)**. Thus, it is obviously important to know the nationality of any historian you quote on this subject!

Answer

Guidance notes

Definition is essential in any discussion of resistance in the Third Reich. 'For more than twenty years, West German resistance historiography was largely preoccupied ... with élite opposition by conservative and bourgeois groups and individuals' (Kershaw). Such opposition was described as 'resistance without the people'; not until the 1970s and 1980s was it possible to conceive of 'resistance by the people'. The emphasis now shifted to the impact of the Nazi regime on everyday life and the examples of conflict and collaboration it produced. The concept of 'resistance' was considerably widened and was now beginning to be categorised into such terms as 'dissent', 'opposition' and 'resistance' – the last denoting a fundamental challenge to the regime. These three categories of resistance will be examined first before an assessment is made of their extent and effects.

Introduction. As the first sentence states, accurate definition of the word **'resistance'** is essential in answering any question on this topic. Here, the terms **'resistance without the people'** and **'resistance by the people'**, together with the three categories of resistance, are introduced straight away. They also help to provide part of the plan for your answer.

Dissent based on material grievances was widespread but, as Noakes and Pridham point out, was basically non-political and the sort of grumbling with which any government has to contend. What might be classified as 'civil disobedience' (refusal to give the 'Heil Hitler' greeting, hanging out church banners rather than the swastika flag, fraternisation with foreign workers) might have a more political tinge but normally went hand in hand with support for much of what the regime was achieving – anti-Bolshevism, an end to unemployment, even anti-Semitism. Such actions might counter the Nazi attempt to control all aspects of society, but they could not threaten the regime.

Quotations. How would you turn this rather lengthy quotation into one of more memorable length, using your own words in indirect speech?

More powerful and effective opposition might have been expected from the Christian churches – 'the only institutions which had an alternative "ideology" to the regime and were permitted to retain their own organisational autonomy' (Noakes and Pridham). But their potential for opposition was weakened by the links between German Protestantism and German nationalism, by the hatred for Bolshevism within the Roman Catholic Church, by the anti-Semitism which affected both churches and by the important benefits which could be derived from collaboration with the state. Thanks to Martin Niemöller and those priests who formed the Confessional Church, the Lutherans maintained their independence, but their efforts to preserve it prevented them from becoming 'the spearhead of political opposition to the Nazis' (Conway). The Roman Catholic Church was similarly intent on protecting the advantages it had gained through the Concordat of July 1935; its opposition was limited to battles over youth groups and the attempt to remove crucifixes from Catholic schools. As in the Lutheran Church, individuals spoke out against Hitler's policies and suffered for it, but there was little response from the majority to Nazi inhumanity and the attack on civil liberties.

Between 1933 and 1939 the main opposition to the regime came from the left. However, the destruction of both political parties and the trade unions had deprived the left of its natural power base and forced it to operate underground with its headquarters abroad. The SPD began by smuggling literature into the country but by 1937 had chosen to concentrate on preserving a nucleus of organisation for a future socialist party. As it became clear that effective opposition by the SPD alone was impossible, some of its underground leaders began to make contact with the army, which represented the only means by which the regime might be removed. The communists were, unsurprisingly, more adept at underground activities, but this did not stop their cells from being ruthlessly eliminated. Doctrinal differences with the socialists and fluctuating policies from Moscow prevented the organisation of any combined movement of the left which might have extended to the mass of the working class.

As is usual in totalitarian regimes, the only real hope of effective resistance lay with the right-wing German establishment, and particularly with the army. The former could destroy Hitler if sufficient high-ranking officers in the latter could be persuaded to stage a military coup, but obstacles abounded: the oath of loyalty to Hitler, the traditional patriotism of the officer class, the need for foreign support, particularly in wartime. In 1938, disquiet over Hitler's foreign policy led to plans for a coup if the Czech crisis should lead to war; the outcome of the Munich Conference ended any hope of success; and Hitler's continued run of diplomatic and military triumphs (1938–41) made further hope of military action untenable. Once the Russian campaign began to turn sour, however, the prospects for the opposition improved and the Kraisau Circle became 'the intellectual powerhouse of the non-communist opposition'. By 1943 a small group of high-ranking officers was planning Hitler's assassination, nearly succeeding in blowing up his aircraft in March 1943. Other plans followed, each unsuccessful, until Count von Stauffenberg reinvigorated the conspiracy and planned 'Operation Valkyrie'. The tragic failure of 20 July 1944 was due partly to the chance moving of the briefcase containing the bomb, but success might still have been possible if the plotters had moved with greater urgency in Berlin and Paris. As it was, the failure of the Bomb Plot destroyed both the German Resistance and the power of the officer corps.

Question. Although it is not described in any detail, the lack of foreign support – particularly in wartime, where the Allied policy of 'unconditional surrender' played a significant part – is obviously an important factor in the failure of German resistance. Should more have been made of it in this paragraph?

How widespread and effective was German resistance in the broadest sense of the term? Considering the truly terrifying nature of the regime and the popularity of many of its measures, 'the extent of defiance – however ineffective – on the part of ordinary Germans cannot fail to impress' (Kershaw). German resistance may ultimately have been ineffective but it cannot truly be described as 'resistance without the people', although the silent majority had indeed earned Sophie Scholl's rebuke at her trial: 'What we have written and said is in the mind of all of you, but you lack the courage to say it aloud.'

Essay 9

Mini essay plan

Paragraph 1

Introduction. Definition of 'resistance' essential. By the 1980s it was categorised in such terms as 'dissent', 'opposition' and 'resistance'.

Paragraph 2

Dissent and 'civil disobedience'.

Paragraph 3

Opposition from the Lutheran and Roman Catholic churches.

Paragraph 4

Opposition from the left – SPD and communists.

Paragraph 5

Resistance from the army – the Bomb Plot.

Paragraph 6

Conclusion. Extent of defiance impresses; although ineffective, it cannot be described as 'resistance without the people'.

General comments

Related questions

1 'No backing from either within or without.' What do you see as the reasons for the failure of the German opposition to Nazi rule?

2 'A noble sacrifice by brave and honourable Germans.' 'A convenient postwar invention.' In the light of these contrasting statements, analyse the motives and the failures of the German resistance to the Hitler regime from 1939 to 1945.

3 Consider the view that 'there is no simple explanation of the outcome of the 20 July 1944 attempt to overthrow Hitler; the causes of the failure can be found in Berlin and in France as well as in East Prussia'.

The specimen essay provides you with plenty of detail on dissent, opposition and resistance. These questions show that a knowledge of **(1)** the degree to which the people continued to support the regime, even in wartime, **(2)** the lack of support from foreign powers, both in peace and war, **(3)** the details of the attempt of 20 July and the reasons for its failure, **(4)** the attitudes of postwar historians to the German resistance, are all essential to cover the likely questions on this topic. If you already have sufficient material to cover these aspects, or have the time to gather it, then this could prove an interesting and valuable **revision topic** with some wider historical implications (see **Williamson**, *Nazism*, **Chapter 14**, and **Kershaw**, *The Nazi Dictatorship*, **Chapter 8**).

Essay 10

Nazi Germany

What conflicting pressures governed Nazi policy towards the Jews between 1933 and 1939?

Tackling the question

Questions on the Holocaust are often divided by the outbreak of World War Two. Here, we concentrate on the period 1933–9. This question is straightforward: it requires you to list the 'conflicting pressures' and, by implication, arrange them in some order of precedence. The two most important are the passionately anti-Semitic views of Hitler, and the similar pressures from below, where the ordinary party members wished to carry out the anti-Jewish policy in which they believed.

Answer

Guidance notes

'Anti-Semitism was the core of Nazi ideology in general and of Hitler's own "world view" in particular' (Noakes and Pridham). In spite of this, there was no detailed programme of anti-Jewish measures which the Nazis could immediately implement when they came to power, apart from a determination 'to exclude the Jews from German life'. To understand the conflicting pressures governing their subsequent policy, it is necessary to examine the details of that developing policy and then to evaluate the pressures which governed it: Hitler's beliefs and Nazi ideology, which fitted well with traditional German anti-Semitism; economic pressures, comprising both dangers to the German economy and the desire of party members to take over Jewish businesses; the part played by individual Nazi leaders and by the party rank and file; finally, the pressures of international opinion and the reactions of the mass of the German people.

During the period 1933–9, Jewish persecution was intermittent, often reacting to the 'revolution from below' but always increasing in severity. The official boycott of Jewish business and professionals (1 April 1933) was a reaction to the spontaneous and local attacks on Jews which followed the election of 5 March. The economic effects and the opposition of Hindenburg limited

Paragraphs. This paragraph describes the progress of Jewish persecution during the period 1933–9, but doesn't lose sight of the 'conflicting pressures', such as the 'revolution from below', reaction to world opinion and the effects in the economic field. Always keep the question in mind, even when you're writing a factual account of a sequence of events.

the action to one day and the apathy of the general public showed it to have been a failure. But action against Jews in the professions provided a safer target, and the Law for the Restoration of the Professional Civil Service (7 April 1933), with its so-called 'Aryan clause', was followed by a similar exclusion of lawyers, doctors and dentists, while the establishment of the Reich Chambers of Culture and the passing of the Editors' Law (4 October 1933) made it easy to exclude Jews from the literary and cultural scene. 1934 was a year of relative calm with no significant anti-Jewish legislation passed, but the former pattern was repeated in 1935 with further outbreaks of local violence against Jews and building pressure on the government to revoke Jewish citizenship and deal with such questions as the definition of Jewishness, mixed marriages and sexual relations outside marriage. The result was the sudden appearance of the Nuremberg Laws (15 September 1935) and subsequent decrees which firmly fixed the Jews as second-class citizens in the Reich. 1936 was the year of the Berlin Olympics and once again there was a halt in Jewish persecution, but further radicalisation of anti-Semitism began in the autumn of 1937. Schacht, 'the main barrier to radical anti-Semitism in the economic field', was replaced by Goering who was ready to encourage the process of 'voluntary' Aryanisation of Jewish firms. A Decree for the Registration of Jewish Property (26 April 1935) foreshadowed its confiscation and the excesses of *Reichskristallnacht* (9 November 1938) paved the way for further decrees excluding Jews from economic life, confiscating all Jewish valuables, excluding Jewish children from schools and, in January 1939, imposing a curfew on all Jews. By the beginning of that year, the SS were in control of anti-Jewish policy, the Central Reich Agency for Jewish Emigration had been established in Berlin under Heidrich, while the outbreak of war 'finally freed the Nazi regime of all tactical restraints and opened the way for the radical solution' (Bracher).

Paragraphs. Although this paragraph deals partly with Hitler's anti-Semitic views, it might have been better to stress them more clearly, while acknowledging that his involvement was intermittent and lacked any evidence of a coherent plan. What do you think?

German anti-Semitism had a history reaching back into the last century and beyond; it has been described as 'the bastard child of the union of Christian anti-Semitism with German nationalism'. Hitler was a willing pupil and anti-Semitism occupied a dominant position in the ideology of the NSDAP and its leaders. But pressure from the Führer during the period 1933–9 was inter- mittent, for he kept a deliberately low profile and, while reacting to demands from below, was ready to heed the limitations imposed by economic realities, international opinion and the reactions of the majority of the German people. There is little sign of any coherent plan: the Nuremberg Laws were announced almost as an afterthought; 'Crystal Night' saw Goebbels as the chief instigator and Goering as the minister who benefited most from the results. But it must always be remembered that all anti-Semitic legislation came with Hitler's approval and that, by 1939, his radical views were chillingly clear, already embracing the extermination of the Jews.

Schacht, until his departure in November 1937, was the main barrier to radical economic measures against the Jews, and he convinced Hitler of the dangers of a foreign boycott of German trade if he yielded to pressure from his supporters for the seizure of Jewish banks and businesses. But without Schacht's warnings and with the evidence of Germany's economic recovery and her stronger international position, Hitler was willing to allow the radical economic moves of 1938 to go ahead, so that 'through Aryanisation, ghettorisation and deportation, the terror against the Jews became part of the Four-Year Plan' (Bracher).

Party members were strongly anti-Semitic and their actions, at local and regional level, with the pressures they exerted on the leadership, had much to do with the 1933 boycott, the Nuremberg Laws and 'Crystal Night'. Personal fears (Goebbels urging revenge for von Rath's murder in order to restore his position with the Führer) and bureaucratic rivalries (Goering's determination to manage anti-Semitic policy and Himmler's successful take-over of that policy by 1939) all added to the gradual radicalisation of anti-Jewish measures. At first Hindenburg and the conservative élite acted as something of a brake, but after the former's death and the growth of the 'Hitler myth', the Establishment counted for little, while Hitler felt strong enough to disregard international protests and limited popular support for the policy.

Paragraphs. There is a lot about 'conflicting pressures' in this paragraph, but possibly not enough on the pressures from below. At least another sentence might restore the balance.

Nazi policy against the Jews was indeed governed by conflicting pressures, but the most demanding came from the Führer himself, although he might be temporarily deflected by other considerations and unwilling to show his hand too clearly.

Conclusion. Do you agree that 'the most demanding [pressure] came from the Führer himself'? In this period, was that stronger than 'pressure from below'? What do you think?

Essay 10

Mini essay plan

Paragraph 1 Introduction. Anti-Semitism the core of Hitler's and Nazi ideology, but no plans for its implementation in 1933.

Paragraph 2 Details of Nazi anti-Jewish policy, 1933–9.

Paragraph 3 Historical German anti-Semitism and Nazi ideology. No coherent plan, but every advance dependent on Hitler's approval.

Paragraph 4 Danger to the German economy an early barrier to a radical policy which eventually became part of the Four-Year Plan.

Paragraph 5 Pressures from party members, the party leadership; the Hitler myth is eventually too strong for establishment opposition.

Paragraph 6 Conclusion. Governed by conflicting pressures above all from Hitler.

General comments

Related questions

1 'Hitler's ideology was the most powerful factor in the shaping of Nazi anti-Semitic policy.' How far is this true of the period 1933–9?

2 'A product of the lack of co-ordination which marked Nazi planning on Jewish policy.' How far do you agree with this view of the events of *Kristallnacht*?

3 How far had Nazi Germany progressed towards a final solution of the 'Jewish problem' by 1939?

Questions 1 and 3 deal with the whole period 1933–9, while **Question 2** is concerned with one incident in that period. (In fact, it is worth noting here that single events, such as *Kristallnacht*, are more often the subject of document questions.) Note also that all three are '**how far...?**' questions. **Question 1**, an obvious **relative importance** question, will use much the same material as the specimen essay, although a paragraph on Hitler's ideology must be added. What other changes will you need to make?

Question 2 highlights another weakness of Nazi planning; it will also require some detailed knowledge of the immediate causes and results of the events of 9/10 November 1938. Such knowledge will be useful to illustrate 'conflicting pressures' in essays on the whole period.

In answering **Question 3**, you can make use of much of the material in the specimen essay, adding a final paragraph to sum up the position reached in 1939.

This seems to be a suitable **revision topic**, in that little extra work will be required to answer likely questions on it, but you should remember that the more common questions on the Holocaust are those dealing with the period 1939–45.

Essay 11

> 'Those who have youth on their side control the future'
> (Hans Schemm, leader of the Nazi Teachers' League).
> How successful was Nazi youth policy in producing
> ideological commitment to the beliefs of the party?

Tackling the question

Questions on Nazi policy towards German youth are not very often set; one is included here because the subject is linked with the general failure of Nazi ideology to take firm root in the minds of the German people and with the concept of a **'social revolution'** in Germany during the 1930s.

Always look carefully at questions including a quotation **to make sure of the exact link** **between quotation and question.** Here, the quotation provides an important reason why Nazi youth policy required 'ideological commitment to the beliefs of the party'; it **does not** touch on the question of how successful party policy was in this field. Careful analysis of this type of question will prevent serious mistakes in planning an answer – it can be remarkably easy to write on the wrong subject!

Answer

Guidance notes

Nazi policy for youth 'aimed to secure the younger generation's total loyalty to the regime and their willingness to fight in the war that lay ahead' (Detlev Penkert). What was the ideology of the regime to which youth was to be committed? Layton finds four strands which stand out from the vague, sometimes contradictory, skein of Nazi ideology: firstly, the importance of racial purity for the superior Aryan peoples, leading to violent anti-Semitism; secondly, the concept of *Volksgemeinschaft* by which all would work together for the good of the nation; thirdly, the need for a one-party state, run on the leadership principle (*Führerprinzip*) in place of the failed democracy of Weimar; lastly, an aggressive nationalism, seeking a Greater Germany. The question of how far German youth was committed to this ideology requires an examination of the salient features of the Hitler Youth (HJ) and of Nazi educational policy, together with the other pressures which affected German youth.

Introduction. The introduction shows that the answer will not only deal with the Hitler Youth movement, but will also consider the part played by schools, universities and the family. You can see why it's so important to think clearly when making your plan; under the pressure of exam conditions it would be easy to seize on the subject of the HJ – particularly if you happen to know quite a lot about that after, say, doing a project on it – and to forget that it was no more than one of the means by which ideological commitment might be produced. Don't rush in.

Since 1900 Germany had been remarkable for the number and diversity of its youth organisations. In 1933 HJ members represented only 1% of all organised youth; by 1938, under the energetic leadership of Baldur von Shirach, 77% of all Germans between the ages of 10 and 18 were in the movement, membership of which was made compulsory in 1939. Some remnants of pre-1933 youth movements remained (the principle that 'Youth must be led by youth'; the 'high ideals of comradeship, loyalty and honour') and participation in youth activities was certainly extended, particularly to girls, but soon the incessant competitiveness, the growing militaristic regimentation, the sometimes brutal discipline and the contempt for intellectual attainment revealed the Nazi ideals which lay below the surface.

Factual evidence. For more information on the **'Swing' movement** and the **'Edelweiss Pirates'**, see the chapter 'Youth in the Third Reich' by **Detlev Peukert**, in **Richard Bessel's** *Life in the Third Reich*. Should a little more information on these important signs of youth rebellion have been included in this paragraph?

What was the impact on German youth? Inevitably, it was mixed, depending on the quality of local leadership and on the individual's response. Parents and teachers resented the interference with studies, over-rapid expansion brought in poor leaders, the activities of Hitler Youth patrols were strongly resented and working-class opposition crystallised in the activities of the 'Edelweiss Pirate' groups, while the more opulent middle classes showed their support for banned foreign jazz in the 'Swing' movement. Thus any success in inculcating Nazi ideology was 'probably limited' (Noakes and Pridham).

The Nazis were well aware that schools and universities were vital in moulding youthful opinion and they were determined that the teachers must be 'politically reliable and ideologically sound'. A thorough purge of teachers was carried out in 1933–4, political references and party vetting sought to provide reliable teachers for the future and the NSLB (their professional association) was also responsible for ideological indoctrination in 8–14 day camps. Many teachers had initially been supporters of the regime, but their association lacked political clout and was dominated by elementary teachers; leading Nazis were hostile and the HJ were bitter rivals. In particular, many were disillusioned by the failure to provide those improvements in the profession promised by the party before 1933.

School organisation was also reformed: control was centralised, three basic models of secondary schools were introduced, private and denominational schools were discriminated against and the introduction of the 'leadership principle' removed democratic decision making. Élite schools appeared: *Napolas*, boarding schools to train a future Nazi élite which soon fell under SS domination; Adolf Hitler Schools, which provided further party control and were open only to Aryans and those with good records in the HJ; *Ordensburgen* ('Castles of the Order') for those who had completed conscription. But in all these the curriculum was too dominated by ideological indoctrination and physical education, so that those who attended them were intellectually restricted. Finally, the school curriculum was made ideologically sound (the chief changes being in German literature, biology and history), but this did nothing to improve the standard of school-leavers.

In higher education, the Nazis wanted a new type of student, teacher and scholarship. Students were forced to join the NSDSTB and had to complete four months' labour service and two months in an SA camp before graduation. At first, many came to terms with the new order, but by the end of the 1930s some were turning against regimentation and conformity. Lecturers were purged (1933–4), with nearly 15% replaced, most seriously in scientific subjects where the figure rose to 18%; there was political vetting of appointments; the leadership principle was applied to destroy democratic self-government. The new scholarship made little headway, with its novel racialist and eugenic ideas, because 'Nazi ideology was so diffuse ... [and] ... so incoherent' and because of the threat to 'science and technology vital to German industry and to the military effort' (Noakes and Pridham).

Quotations. This rather 'messy' quotation (from the point of view of punctuation) would be better expressed in your own words in indirect speech. Try changing it.

Finally, it must not be forgotten that German youth also suffered from other pressures: from Nazi policies on the family, religion and the place of women in society and from the effects of ceaseless propaganda and the threat from the Gestapo. The Nazis might regard the family as the 'germ-cell of the nation', but their over-riding concern with the cult of prolific motherhood produced strains in the family which were greatly increased by the teachings of the HJ (producing ten-year-olds who 'entertained vastly inflated notions of their self-importance') and by parents' fears of denunciation to the Gestapo.

How great, then, was the ideological commitment of the young? Hitler, at the end of his life, believed that he had failed 'to form a youth imbued deeply with National Socialist doctrine'; nevertheless, Bullock stresses, the German people continued to fight an increasingly hopeless war until Hitler's death brought a belated surrender. A survey by the American occupying forces in Dorm-stadt in 1945 found 42% of those under 19 believing that German reconstruction needed 'a strong new Führer'. The Hitler myth had always been more potent than party ideology, but the Nazis had failed to keep sufficient youth on their side to control the future.

Mini essay plan

Paragraph 1	Introduction. Four strands of Nazi ideology.
Paragraph 2	The growth of the HJ movement.
Paragraph 3	The impact of the HJ movement on German youth.
Paragraph 4	Nazi policy towards teachers in schools.
Paragraph 5	Nazi reforms in school organisation; élite schools; reform of the curriculum.
Paragraph 6	Nazi reforms in higher education: new teachers, new students, new scholarship.
Paragraph 7	Pressures on the young within the family, from propaganda and from terror.
Paragraph 8	Conclusion. The Hitler myth more potent than party ideology; the Nazis had failed to keep sufficient youth on their side to control the future.

General comments

Related questions

1 How effectively did the Nazi regime mobilise support among women and young people between 1933 and 1945?

2 How successfully did the Nazi regime attempt to transform the nature of family life in Germany?

3 Why did Nazi ideology fail to take root in the minds of the majority of the German people?

Questions on Nazi policy towards the youth of Germany are often combined with those on similar lines dealing with other groups in the population. In **Question 1**, youth policy is allied with the policy towards women – the most obvious 'pairing'. In **Question 2**, a question on 'family life' will include much of the same material. If you're going to choose youth policy as a **revision topic**, you should also include other groups which might be allied with it in questions: women, the family, the working class, etc. These will also help to answer questions on whether or not the Nazis achieved a 'social revolution'.

The answer to **Question 3** will need to examine critically various aspects of Nazi ideology before looking at the reactions of different groups such as those described above.

A possible **revision topic**, but one which requires work on several different subjects. If you're considering revising the Nazi attainment of a **'social revolution'**, then you might well add this topic – the two are complementary.

Essay 12

How far are you convinced by the arguments of those who see the 'Final Solution' as a haphazard attempt to improvise a policy in the chaos of wartime Europe rather than as a culmination of Hitler's political career and beliefs?

Tackling the question

The second specimen essay on the Holocaust. Although this is a **'how far...?'** question, it also clearly demands a choice between two clearly expressed views on the subject. In other words, it is also a **discussion** question. The advantages of long questions are again apparent: the detail given in the question ensures that you can see exactly what is required in the answer, if you're familiar with the two sides of the historical argument over the development of Nazi anti-Semitic policy during World War Two. Once again, **Kershaw**, *The Nazi Dictatorship*, **Chapter 5**, provides a detailed coverage of this continuation of the 'Intentionalist v Structuralist' controversy; **Lee, Williamson** and **Layton** give much shorter accounts.

Answer

Two schools of historical thought have emerged on the subject of Hitler and the Final Solution and these correspond to the 'Intentionalists' and 'Structuralists' of other debates – the former being those who support a Hitler-centred interpretation of the Third Reich and the latter those who play down the significance of Hitler and focus attention on the structure of the Nazi state, emphasising the complexities of the regime and its decision-making processes. In terms of anti-Semitic policy, the argument centres on whether 'the Final Solution had its origins in Hitler's mind' (Davidowicz) and 'happened because Hitler willed it' (Layton) or whether, with no written evidence for a direct 'Führer Order' for the policy, its being put into effect is by no means to be ascribed to Hitler alone, but to the complexity of the decision-making process in the Third Reich, which brought about a 'progressive and cumulative radicalisation' (Mommsen). An account of the progress made towards the 'Final Solution' is a necessary preliminary to a reasoned judgement between these two arguments.

Guidance notes

Introduction. The introduction is used to expand the two arguments which are to be discussed. The plan of this essay can be taken as a model for dealing with **discussion** questions of this type. After an introduction defining the arguments to be discussed: **(1)** give an account of the facts, **(2)** set out the arguments on both sides, **(3)** discuss the strong and weak points of each argument, **(4)** produce a conclusion – often a synthesis of the two arguments, as in this case.

'It was the approach of war that heralded the opening of a new stage in Hitler's attitude to the Jewish question' (Bullock). As Kershaw stresses, the emigration of Jews remained the main aim at the start of the war; what was altered were the 'possibilities of its implementation'. The rapid conquest of Poland brought the additional problem of three million Polish Jews and 'the process of radicalisation ... gathered momentum between 1939 and 1941'. The forced expulsion of Jews from north-west Poland to the *Generalgouvernement* – the remainder of German-occupied Poland – 'led unavoidably to the establishment of ghettos' and with the introduction of compulsory labour for all Jews 'provided part of the momentum which was later to culminate in the Final Solution' (Kershaw). Emigration to some 'reservation' – possibly Madagascar – was still being discussed in 1940, but it was the start of Operation Barbarossa which marked what Christopher Browning described as a 'quantum jump' in anti-Jewish policy. This was the mass-shootings of Russian Jews by the *SS-Einsatzgruppen* as they advanced behind the Panzer armies. Although no written evidence survives, it seems likely that Hitler had taken a decision to exterminate the Jews shortly before Göring's directive to Heindrich (31 July 1941). Whenever the decision was taken, it still had to be implemented in what Bullock describes as 'the industrialisation of mass murder', and the memo issued after the Wannsee Conference (20 January 1942) describes as the 'combing of Europe from west to east'. The whole vast and crazy plan was then under way and was to be continued until the Soviet advance began to overrun the death camps in 1944.

The Intentionalist thesis is immediately attractive. Throughout his political life, Hitler made no secret of his hatred for the Jews, although he was careful to use what Davidowicz calls 'esoteric language'. Few would question Bullock's claim that 'Hitler alone had the imagination – however twisted – to come up with such a plan [the extermination of the whole of European Jewry]'. Hitler also legitimised the Final Solution: his followers had no doubt they were obeying his intentions, while the absence of a written 'Führer Order' could be explained by the need for secrecy. It is easy to be convinced that extermination 'grew out of the bioligistic insanity of Nazi ideology' (Bracher) and that, whatever the precise timing of the various steps in the programme, it was in accordance with what was in the forefront of Hitler's mind throughout his life.

The Structuralist explanation sees the Final Solution as 'the end product of a cumulative process of radicalisation ... beginning in a series of separate massacres and ... issuing in a solution which becomes institutionalised' (Bullock) with 'Hitler as catalyst but not the decision-maker' (Browning). Such an explanation does address the question of how, in less than a decade, a political system can become 'so corrupted that it regards the implementation of genocide as one of its supreme tasks, [thus] turning a slogan of "get rid of the Jews" into a programme of annihilation' (Kershaw). It may also be noted that the Structuralist approach reveals more of the part played by such active collaborators as the SS, the Wehrmacht, the civil service and German industry, and allocates more widely the guilt which Intentionalists see as primarily belonging to Hitler.

Both theories have their weaknesses. For the Intentionalist, Hitler's part in directly influencing policy is often hard to detect; he seems rather to be sanctioning and legitimising the initiatives of others. Indeed, before 1941 there is little evidence that Hitler had anything more than a vague conviction that Jews must be 'got rid of' from Germany and even from Europe – this hardly equates with the long-term 'plan' or 'programme' which the Intentionalists claim to have discovered. Similarly, the Structuralist approach seems often to neglect the ideological drive and decision making at the top, without which the Final Solution would not have occurred. Moreover, as Fox has indicated, if the 'physical extermination of Soviet Jewry ... was undertaken for obvious ideological reasons', why is it claimed that 'the extermination of European Jewry was begun simply because of administrative "inconvenience"'?

As with many post-1945 historical debates, the truth lies somewhere between the two extremes. Without Hitler's insane racial theories and his obsessive drive to put them into practice there would have been no 'Final Solution'; equally, without the active co-operation of the Wehrmacht, the SS and many civilians and foreigners, without local initiatives in the organisational chaos of Nazi Europe, without the ambitions of an Eichmann and the sadistic brutality of the executioners, the plans of the Führer would have come to nothing.

Quotations. The two longer quotations in this paragraph are valuable; can you make them shorter and more memorable by putting them in your own words as indirect speech?

Mini essay plan

Paragraph 1	Introduction. 'Intentionalists' and 'Structuralists'.
Paragraph 2	Sequence of events 1939–45.
Paragraph 3	The Intentionalist case.
Paragraph 4	The Structuralist case.
Paragraph 5	Criticisms of both arguments.
Paragraph 6	Conclusion. Synthesis is required.

General comments

Related questions

1 With what justification has it been argued that the decision to launch the 'Final Solution' in 1941–2 was not the result of deliberate long-term planning but a confused response to short-term considerations?

2 When and why did the leaders of the Third Reich commit themselves to the policy known as the 'Final Solution'?

3 'The destruction of the Jews reveals with particular clarity the true nature of the National Socialist state.' Discuss.

These three questions on the same topic repay careful analysis. Question 1 is a carbon copy of the specimen essay question. It should not be necessary to alter the plan at all.

Question 2 uses the common 'when and why?' formula, with the 'when' part of more importance and with much more contradictory evidence than is usually the case. The 'why' part should follow the lines of the specimen essay; in fact, the only difference would be the insertion of a paragraph dealing with the timing of the start of the 'Final Solution', with a consequent shortening of the second paragraph.

Question 3 is a good question because it should make the candidate think about the answer and not jump too quickly to a conclusion. At first sight, the question appears to take a **'Structuralist'** view of the Holocaust, but a little thought will show that an **'Intentionalist'** slant is apparent when one considers the connection between the National Socialist state and the ideology of its Führer. The **MEP** will need some recasting, but much of the material for an answer is there.

We have a good **revision topic** here, but it should be revised alongside Nazi policy towards the Jews between 1933 and 1939. Together they are very likely to provide you with a question in most papers.

Essay 13

Why was Nazi Germany at war with Britain and France in September 1939 and not in September 1938?

Tackling the question

Another **'Why then rather than then?'** type of question **(see Nazi Germany, Essay 3)**. Here the question of **balance** is particularly important: the second part of the question might require you to examine Hitler's foreign policy from 1933 to 1938, while the first part centres on the culmination of the much shorter period between the Munich Conference and the outbreak of World War Two. I've used three paragraphs to cover the period 1933–8, and two shorter ones to discuss the post-Munich events (I suggest you keep to the normal chronological sequence in your answer, although the question reverses this). Do you think the balance is about right?

Answer

Guidance notes

The events of September 1938 leading up to the Munich Conference at the end of that month have aroused much greater historical controversy than the events of 1939, which led to the outbreak of war on 3 September. It might well be argued, however, that Munich was only the culmination of a lengthy policy of appeasement while the guarantee to Poland, which led to the declaration of war by Britain and France, represented a remarkable 'U-turn' in British policy and a decisive repudiation of appeasement. To discover the reasons for the coming of war in 1939 and its avoidance in 1938, it is necessary to consider the foreign policies of Germany, Britain and France up to September 1938; the events which culminated in the Munich settlement; the post-Munich policies of these countries, leading up to the guarantee to Poland; and, finally, the events of August 1939 which led to the outbreak of war.

The defeat of Germany in World War One and the disappearance of the empires of Russia, Austria-Hungary and Turkey left a power vacuum in central Europe which could be filled by a resurgent Germany, whose great manpower and economic

Drill for changing question analysis into MEP. Here we can practise the drill for producing an MEP with a different type of question from that used in **Nazi Germany, Essays 4 and 6**. **(1)** The question becomes: 'Why did Germany not fight Britain and France in 1938 and why did she do so in 1939?' **(2)** The **'gut-reaction'** is that in 1938, Britain and France were desperate to get out of their treaty obligations to Czechoslovakia and were ready to betray the Czechs; Hitler wanted war, but was persuaded to take the Sudeten lands without it. In 1939, Hitler was determined to invade Poland; this time the Allies were, unwillingly, ready to fight to prevent him. **(3) Three facts to support each proposition**. In the case of the first proposition: Hitler had always been set on westward expansion, but was ready to settle, unwillingly, for the Sudeten lands at Munich; Britain was following a policy of appeasement, above all because she could not fight a war on more than one front; political and economic weakness had also turned France towards appeasement; both countries were determined to get out of their treaty obligations to the Czechs. In the case of the second proposition: Hitler was even more determined on war with Poland, and had secured Soviet neutrality by the Nazi–Soviet Pact; he refused to believe that England and France would fight; the Allies had at last abandoned appeasement when Hitler took Prague in March 1939, and were ready as a last resort to declare war on Germany. **(4)** These pieces of evidence can be incorporated in a chronological essay plan, as I've done.

potential made her recovery almost certain. The Weimar governments of the 1920s had already begun the revision of the Versailles settlement which was essential to that recovery; Hitler's immediate aims in 1933 were to continue this process, to seek the friendship of Britain and Italy and to weaken France wherever possible. When he called the (Hossbach) conference of 5 November 1937, the situation had been transformed: France was no longer the dominant power in Europe; Italy was at the other end of the Rome–Berlin Axis; the Four-Year Plan had been established to create a war economy. Historians may disagree about the importance of Hitler's revelations in his speech at this conference; few would deny that it 'marks the point at which the expansion of the Third Reich ceased to be latent and became explicit' (Mason). The *Anschluss* with Austria was the first fruit of this explicit expansion and the consequent encirclement of western Czechoslovakia paved the way for the second.

Britain and France answered this threatening expansionism with appeasement, defined as removing reasons for war by the satisfaction of legitimate demands. The roots of British appeasement lay in popular dislike of a treaty deemed to be unfair, an anti-French and pro-German bias, a genuine hatred of war and, above all, the impossibility of fighting a future war in three different theatres against Germany, Italy and Japan. France's apparent domination of Europe in the 1920s resulted from the weakness of its rivals; in the next decade the effects of economic crisis, social unrest and the failure of the Popular Front all served to produce support for appeasement. Nor was it a foolish policy to pursue in order to gain time for rearmament, providing that potential aggressors would agree to provide something in return for their gains.

The Czech crisis of 1938 and its finale in the Munich Conference has been rightly seen as the culmination of appeasement. Chamberlain had no wish to fight for Czechoslovakia, and the French had even less, although Chamberlain was ignorant of this fact. What was only too clear was the existence of a treaty between France and Czechoslovakia which threatened to draw the former, and her ally Britain, into war with Germany. Chamberlain was thus principally concerned to 'get France off the hook'. Hitler, on the other hand, was determined both to welcome the Sudeten Germans into the Reich and to 'smash Czechoslovakia by military action'. Munich may thus be regarded as a defeat for Hitler: he felt cheated of a military victory and saw the outcome as an attempt by the western powers to limit his ambitions in eastern Europe. But it was still Hitler who drew back from the brink and grudgingly accepted a diplomatic rather than a military solution.

After Munich, Hitler awaited the right moment to deal with the hated Czechs. He planned to use Slovak calls for autonomy as he had used the Sudeten Germans; he reasoned that Britain and France could avoid their guarantees given at Munich if the Czech state could be shown to have disintegrated. But the take-over had unexpected repercussions: Chamberlain eventually taking a hard line and pledging resistance to further German aggression after public opinion was seen to be turning against Germany. Far more important than the Birmingham speech of 17 March was the guarantee offered to Poland by both Britain and France on 31 March: it has subsequently been condemned as a 'blank cheque' given to an anti-Semitic right-wing military dictatorship, 'notorious for its reckless diplomacy' (Farmer). This startling reversal of western policy only served to anger Hitler and persuade him to order preparations for war with Poland by the end of August.

Factual evidence. Given the importance of the 'U-turn' in Allied policy after March 1939, do you think that enough evidence has been provided to explain it? If not, what more might be included?

Both sides now courted the Soviet alliance which was the key to the success of their different policies. The signing of the Nazi–Soviet Pact destroyed the guarantee to Poland; Hitler could never understand how Britain and France could continue with such a hopeless policy. In spite of last-minute doubts he was determined to invade Poland, and the threatened response of Britain and France, although clearly stated, was not enough to deter him.

Thus Hitler unwillingly avoided war in 1938 through Chamberlain's efforts to rescue France from her treaty obligations to Czechoslovakia; war came in 1939 because the same western powers had given a doubtful guarantee to Poland and refused to abandon it when Hitler struck.

Mini essay plan

Paragraph 1   Introduction. Munich the culmination of appeasement; the Polish guarantee represented a 'U-turn' in western policy.

Paragraph 2   German foreign policy, 1933–8.

Paragraph 3   The roots of appeasement.

Paragraph 4   The Czech crisis and the Munich Conference.

Paragraph 5   Post-Munich policies and the guarantee to Poland.

Paragraph 6   The search for a Soviet alliance and the Nazi–Soviet Pact.

Paragraph 7   Conclusion. Chamberlain's efforts to 'get France off the hook' forced the unwilling Hitler to avoid war in 1938; war came in 1939 because Britain and France refused to abandon the Polish guarantee.

General comments

Related questions

1 How would you allocate responsibility for the crisis of international relations in Europe in 1939?

2 'Nazi foreign policy from 1933 to 1939 followed consistent principles but by increasingly reckless means.' How valid do you find this verdict?

3 'The key diplomatic event of 1939 was not the Munich Crisis of September 1938 but the Nazi–Soviet Pact, signed in August.' Do you agree?

Questions on the diplomatic events of 1939, leading up to the start of World War Two, are usually concerned, either directly or indirectly, with the aims and methods of Nazi Germany, Britain and France, Italy and the Soviet Union. If your paper is one on Nazi Germany, your essay answers will concentrate on the aims and methods of that country; if it is an 'Outlines' paper on Europe in the 1930s, more weight will have to be given to the aims and methods of the other players. In **Question 1**, it is important not to over-emphasise Hitler's responsibility. **Question 2** deals with German principles and means: the key questions are how consistent were they and did recklessness increase? **Question 3** provides a direct choice between the importance of two events; in such questions, it may be necessary to admit that it is impossible to rank the events in order. To do so is not a sign of weakness!

Essay 14

Would you agree that World War Two was 'Hitler's War'?

Tackling the question

Y ou couldn't have a much shorter question than this! The phrase **'Hitler's War'** has come to be used to sum up the views of the **'Intentionalists'** (and where have we met them before?) who see Hitler as 'the final arbiter', if not 'the chief animator' of Nazi foreign policy. Their other name, **'Programmists'**, stresses the existence of a programme in Hitler's mind to which he stuck throughout the 1930s.

Against them stand the **'Structuralists/ anti-Programmists'**, who find no programme but rather the work of a supreme opportunist in pre-World War Two events. Don't think that the existence of such opposite views requires you to take one side or the other; **Bullock's** conclusion may well be the right answer, but there is much more agreement that without Hitler there would have been no war (see **Fest**, *Hitler*, **pages 607–21**).

Answer

Guidance notes

As Stephen Lee points out, 'the Nuremberg Judgment maintained that the Second World War was the outcome of Nazi policy and of Hitler's determination not to depart from the course he had set himself'. Not surprisingly, some postwar historians have been critical of this conclusion: to investigate its truth, it will be necessary to consider the situation in Europe after 1918; the evidence for a change in traditional German foreign policy under Hitler (particularly the importance of the so-called Hossbach Memorandum); the arguments which divide 'Intentionalists' and 'Structuralists' and their differing views of Hitler's foreign policy; the question of how far German foreign policy, 1933–9, was indeed Hitler's policy; and, finally, the degree of responsibility of other countries for the outbreak of war in 1939.

The situation in Europe at the end of World War One was not nearly as depressing for Germany as the terms of the Versailles settlement might indicate. The disappearance of the Russian, Austro-Hungarian and Turkish empires had created a power vacuum in central and eastern Europe which could be filled by a

Drill for changing question analysis into MEP. (1) Was Hitler the chief cause of World War Two? **(2)** 'Gut-reaction' – 'yes, he was!' **(3)** Germany's post-World War One situation; Hitler's foreign policy up to the Hossbach Conference and the change thereafter; how far was German foreign policy Hitler's policy?; how far was Hitler's foreign policy influenced by other states; how far were their actions a cause of World War Two?; the views of Intentionalists versus those of Structuralists; **(4)** the order of these six points has been changed in the final essay plan in order to use the Hossbach Conference as an introduction to the Intentionalist v. Structuralist paragraph.

resurgent Germany. The USSR was too new and too delicate to play the great power, Britain and France had been decisively weakened by the effects of war, while the USA had retreated into isolationism and a refusal to uphold the new European order that Wilson had done so much to create. In such a situation, Germany's great manpower and economic potential made her recovery almost certain; indeed, the revision of the Versailles settlement had already begun under the Weimar governments.

Factual evidence. The big criticism of this essay is that it doesn't describe the events leading up to the outbreak of World War Two but stops at the Hossbach Conference and the change in direction of Nazi foreign policy that it marks. A paragraph covering Munich, the Anglo-French Polish guarantee and the Nazi–Soviet Pact is surely necessary. How would you fit this in without increasing the length of the essay?

When he gained power in 1933, Hitler's immediate aims were to continue to break free from the restrictions of the Versailles treaty, to end German isolation by seeking the friendship of Britain and Italy and to weaken France wherever possible. By the end of 1936, there had been a remarkable change in Germany's position in Europe. France was no longer the dominant European power, most of the Versailles restrictions had been removed and Mussolini's Italy was now at the other end of the Rome–Berlin Axis. Faced with an economic crisis in the autumn of 1936, Hitler had established the Four-Year Plan to create a war economy. At the end of the following year he called the conference which has assumed the name of his adjutant who took the minutes. Historians have been divided over its significance – Taylor sees Hitler as 'day-dreaming' while the Nuremberg judges found a blueprint for aggression in his speech – but most would now probably agree with Mason that 'the conference marks the point at which the expansion of the Third Reich ceased to be latent and became explicit', while the opposition of Neurath, Fritsch and Blomberg caused all three to lose their jobs.

Arguments over the Hossbach Memorandum illustrate the gulf dividing the 'Intentionalists/Programmists' (who see Hitler's foreign policy as based on statements in *Mein Kampf, Hitler's Secret Book* and his *Table Talk* and as remaining 'remarkably consistent ... in spite of his flexible approach to details') and the 'Structuralists/anti-Programmists' (who question 'whether National Socialist foreign policy can be considered an unchanging pursuit of established priorities', and who see Hitler as a pragmatist, a successful opportunist, with a policy shaped by 'agencies and institutions, both inside and outside the party', by powerful individuals such as Goering and Ribbentrop, by economic and domestic pressures, even by nothing more than 'expansion without object' and dominated by considerations of prestige and propaganda). As with the parallel arguments over domestic and anti-Semitic policies in the Third Reich, the truth lies somewhere between the two extremes, for example in Bullock's conception of 'consistency of aim with complete opportunism in method and tactics' and Kershaw's conclusion that 'Hitler's ideological aims were one important factor in deciding the contours of German foreign policy ... [but] ... it is usually impossible to distinguish them analytically ... [from] ... strategic power-political considerations and ... economic interest'.

Consideration must also be given to the question of how far German foreign policy was Hitler's policy. For the 'Intentionalist' it obviously was; the 'Structuralist' will give more weight to other influences: the expansionist demands of the German ruling class, 'the need to preserve and uphold the domestic social order', or Germany's economic problems of the late 1930s. But Kershaw does not see Hitler as the captive of the German élites and finds that 'foreign and domestic policy were so fused that it seems quite misplaced to speak of a primacy of one over the other'. Milan Hauner goes so far as to see Hitler's role in foreign policy as 'not only the final arbiter but also its chief animator', and it seems certain that 'the broad lines of policy were determined in all cases by Hitler himself' (Kershaw).

Finally, how far was Hitler's foreign policy influenced by the actions of other states? Did the supporters of 'appeasement' accelerate, even ensure, the outbreak of World War Two? It could be argued that the actions of Chamberlain and others, culminating in the surrender of the Sudeten lands at Munich, caused Hitler to mistake 'forbearance in the interests of peace for weakness and diplomatic capitulation' (Lee), and that the sudden switch to guaranteeing Poland would never have convinced Hitler of its seriousness. But it would seem that firmer action, even over the Rhineland, might only have postponed war or, taken at Munich, might have produced war in 1938, possibly to the advantage of Britain and France.

It is clear that the Second World War was indeed 'Hitler's War' in that his actions, combining a long-term programme with short-term opportunism, were the primary, if not the only, cause of the war which began in 1939.

Essay 14

Mini essay plan

Paragraph 1   Introduction. The theory that World War Two was 'Hitler's War' and the criticisms which have been made of this.

Paragraph 2   A favourable situation for Germany in 1918.

Paragraph 3   The importance of the Hossbach Conference.

Paragraph 4   Arguments of 'Intentionalists' and 'Structuralists'.

Paragraph 5   German foreign policy as Hitler's policy?

Paragraph 6   Influence of the actions of other states.

Paragraph 7   Conclusion. World War Two was 'Hitler's War'.

Related questions

1 'Consistency of aim with complete opportunism in method and tactics' (Bullock). Discuss this assessment of Hitler's foreign policy.

2 'Hitler did not make plans – for world conquest or for anything else. He assumed that others would provide opportunities, and that he would seize them' (Taylor). Discuss.

3 'The Second World War was Hitler's personal war in many senses. He intended it, he prepared for it, he chose the moment for launching it' (Trevor-Roper). Discuss.

General comments

If the quotation in your question was written by a famous historian, don't think that you have to agree with it! You can be sure that it represents only one of two or more contradictory views – your job is to discuss them.

Question 1 represents the compromise view between the extremes of the **Intentionalists** and their opponents. It's the one which the specimen essay supports; how far will you need to change the plan of that to answer this question? You'll need to provide more evidence for both claims about Hitler's policy.

Question 2 sets out **Taylor's Structuralist view**; you'll need much the same evidence to discuss it as you'll use in **Question 1**.

In **Question 3**, **Trevor-Roper** sees World War Two as **'Hitler's War'** and takes an obviously **Intentionalist** line. Here, you'll need to follow the plan which the question suggests: intention, preparation, choice of moment for launching war. How will you adapt the specimen essay?

In all, Nazi foreign policy is a good **revision topic**, provided that you do not get lost in the details.

Essay 15

Estimate Hitler's responsibility for Germany's defeat in World War Two.

Tackling the question

The last essay! Another **relative importance** question. How does Hitler's responsibility for Germany's defeat compare with the other reasons for that occurrence?

If you look at the **MEP** and read the specimen essay, you'll see a clear matter for debate. I've concentrated on the German General Staff as the only other responsible factor besides the very obvious shortcomings of their Commander-in-Chief.

Should some mention have been made of the part played by the Allied forces and their commanders in what was also an Allied victory? What of economic factors on both sides? Was Hitler fighting the wrong war as well as fighting it in the wrong way?

Remember that, however strong your **'gut-reaction'** to this question is that Hitler's responsibility outweighed all others, you must still examine other possible reasons for German defeat.

Answer

Guidance notes

Hitler's official war diarist, Percy Schramm, observed that 'the war consolidated his [Hitler's] dictatorship over the military'. Sir Basil Liddell Hart finds that the German generals were 'the best-finished product of their profession – anywhere', but 'they tended to conduct war more in the manner of chess than as an art ... Hitler had the flair that is the characteristic of genius, though accompanied by liability to make elementary mistakes', and he could appreciate the value of new ideas, new weapons and new talent. This combination of high efficiency and flair produced the remarkable series of victories between 1939 and 1941, but the jealousy and inevitable clashes of opinion, which became more obvious as the victories ebbed, widened the differences within the hitherto successful partnership and led eventually to the defeat and disgrace of the General Staff after the Bomb Plot. An estimation of Hitler's part in this process requires an examination of his prewar relationship with the armed forces, an evaluation of the successes and failures of his military decisions and some analysis of events on the Home Front and in economic and diplomatic affairs.

Factual evidence. As has already been pointed out, there's a strong body of opinion which holds that Hitler 'stumbled into war at this time contrary to his plans'. **Fest**, in his biography of Hitler, sees him 'throwing aside more than tried and tested tactics, that he was giving up a policy in which he had excelled for fifteen years and in which for a while he had outstripped all antagonists'. But this was not so much a break with the past as a return to 'the immutable core in Hitler's nature ... his urge for war was so compelling that he not only conceded to reverse his fundamental design but went into the conflict in spite of inadequate preparation' (see **Fest**, *Hitler*, **Interpolation III**, **'The Wrong War'**).

Hitler's relations with the German army were always uneasy. Senior officers saw him as a social and military upstart, but they lacked unity in opposition and were unable to stand up to Hitler as a body. Moreover, they had much to be grateful for: rearmament, an end to the demeaning restrictions of the Versailles treaty, the defeat of the rival SA in 1934. Political intrigue removed Fritsch and Blomburg in 1928; the ensuing reorganisation left Hitler as Commander-in-Chief of the armed forces, the War Ministry was abolished and its powers were transferred to the newly created OKW headed by the pliant General Keitel, the indecisive Brauchitsch becoming Commander-in-Chief of the army and sixteen senior generals losing their jobs. By 1939, Hitler's diplomatic triumphs had won him considerable support within the army and effective resistance from a disunited General Staff was increasingly unlikely.

The dramatic victories in Poland, France and the Balkans (1939–41) hastened the process by which the General Staff were becoming mere 'instruments of the Führer's will'. But even in his most successful period as military leader, Hitler committed important errors. The halting of the Panzer advance on Dunkirk, which allowed a successful evacuation to proceed, and the subsequent quarrels over 'Sea Lion' between the army and navy, with Hitler making little attempt to intervene, both raise the question of how strong a will to defeat Britain actually existed.

The decision to invade the Soviet Union in 1941 was Hitler's most crucial mistake. It began the dreaded two-front war – although Michael Howard has correctly thrown doubt on whether Britain actually posed any real threat in 1941; it was basically begun for ideological reasons, whatever Hitler might claim in public; finally, Hitler made the mistake of under-estimating Soviet forces, making the invasion 'an offensive gamble without precedent in modern history' (Liddell Hart).

Punctuation. A final example of a list, separated by commas, and summed-up with a final dash.

A late start, the appalling Soviet roads which slowed the Panzers' advance, the lack of tracked vehicles which prevented movement when autumn rains turned those roads to mud, the decision to switch the main thrust to the south before continuing the advance on Moscow, finally the advent of the most severe Soviet winter ever recorded and the unexpected counter-attack (5 December 1941), beginning on the very day that Gudarian halted his advance – all these provided good reasons for the failure of the first phase of Hitler's gamble. Little blame can be attached to his actions as Commander-in-Chief during this period – indeed his refusal to permit withdrawal once the advance was halted may well have prevented 'a retreat turning into a rout' (Bullock). But now that *Blitzkrieg* strategy had received its first setback, Hitler began to lose his magic touch. It was foolish to declare war on the USA after Pearl Harbor when it might have been possible to confine the new conflict to the Pacific; it was disastrous to over-extend German lines of communication during the 1942 operations in the southern USSR; it was supreme folly to refuse to withdraw the 6th Army from Stalingrad for the winter and then to deny von Paulus an attempt to break out or even surrender. Now the Soviet war must become defensive, but Hitler was beginning to lose touch with reality as he insisted on continuing the creation of his new racial order in the East. The failure of the Bomb Plot meant that the influence of the General Staff was finally negated by the Nazification of the army, while Hitler's determination to fight on when the war was obviously lost seems to owe more to his belief that the destruction of Germany was a just reward for the failures of the German people than to his exaggerated trust in new weapons or Allied disunity.

At home, the Reich government became even more of a 'battlefield for contending factions' as the Führer became immersed in running the war; reliance on short *Blitzkriegs* and the failure of Goering's Four-Year Plan prevented any full-scale mobilisation of the German war effort before Todt and Speer took over; 'Hitler's short-lived European empire was an improvised structure in which pragmatic and ideological policies vied with each other' (Williamson), after his failure, in the autumn of 1940, to build a united Europe under German leadership.

Thus Hitler's strategy was based on huge and irresponsible risks; he was incapable of organising military retreats, finding 'the defensive role utterly distasteful' (Lee); he lacked the training to command armies in large-scale operations, being too often willing to disregard logistic problems and to become preoccupied with minor details rather than the overall strategic situation. Above all, it was his fatal fixation on the defeat of the Soviet Union which epitomises his responsibility for Germany's defeat.

Conclusion. Few writers would dispute the claim that the invasion of the Soviet Union was the greatest cause of German defeat. Would you agree with the other points made in this conclusion, or would you prefer to accentuate some other features of Hitler's wartime leadership?

Mini essay plan

Paragraph 1	Introduction. Early victories came from a combination of Hitler's flair and the high efficiency of the General Staff.
Paragraph 2	Hitler's prewar relations with the German armed forces.
Paragraph 3	Hitler's errors in the period 1939–41.
Paragraph 4	The decision to invade the Soviet Union as Hitler's most crucial mistake.
Paragraph 5	Hitler's failures during the remainder of the war.
Paragraph 6	Failures on the Home Front, in economic management and in the control of the German empire in Europe.
Paragraph 7	Conclusion. Hitler's failures, particularly his fixation with the Soviet Union, make him primarily responsible for Germany's defeat.

General comments

Related questions

1 'Once the USSR and the USA were united against him, the defeat of Hitler's Germany was merely a matter of time.' Do you agree?

2 'Hitler learnt nothing from his early success; Stalin, by contrast, learned everything from his initial failures.' How far do you agree with this conclusion on the leaders of Germany and the USSR as wartime commanders?

3 Account for the initial success and eventual failure of German *Blitzkrieg* tactics in the Second World War.

As with other **revision topics**, you should check with past papers on the likelihood of questions on World War Two appearing in whichever paper you're entered for. If you're concentrating on the history of Nazi Germany, you may feel that they're not a worthwhile **revision topic**.

The answer to **Question 1** must be to agree with its proposition, unless you can mount a convincing case for a possible German victory after the Grand Alliance had been formed. You might also confront the question of why that defeat took so long.

Both **Question 1** and **Question 2** require a good knowledge of the events and strategy of the war, while the latter also needs a clear picture of Stalin as generalissimo. **Question 2** would only appear in an 'Outlines' paper. Similarly, **Question 3** requires familiarity with *Blitzkrieg* strategy and tactics and with the means by which they would eventually be countered. Some basic knowledge of **military history** is, of course, necessary for most questions on wars.

Source-Based Exercises

Exercise 1

The Abyssinian Crisis

Study Documents I, II, III and IV below and then answer questions (a) to (f) which follow.

Document I

The speedier our action the less likely will be the danger of diplomatic complications. In the Japanese 1
fashion there will be no need whatever officially for a declaration of war and in any case we must
always emphasise the purely defensive character of operations. No one in Europe would raise any
difficulties provided the prosecution of operations resulted rapidly in an accomplished fact. It would
suffice to declare to England and France that their interests would be recognised.   5

Memorandum by Mussolini for Marshal Badoglio, 30 December 1934

Document II

Monsieur Laval ... emphasised that Geneva would accept whatever France and Great Britain
approved. If there were to be an exception it would no doubt be Moscow. As regards peace conditions
the Italian pretensions were excessive, but the British reservations were too severe. Mussolini must
have at least a part of the territory he had conquered.

    Sir Samuel Hoare emphasised that it was essential not to offer the appearance of rewarding 10
aggression ... The cession of territory by Ethiopia in the north must depend for its extent upon
what was done in the south and southwest ... To go too far would lead to the Emperor's overthrow
and provoke the accusation that all the League had managed to do was to ruin Abyssinia.

Record of the Hoare–Laval meeting, 7 December 1935

Document III

Five months before the pretext found in December in the Wal-Wal incident, Italy had begun the
armament of her colonies, armament which has since been intensified and increased by the 15
continuous sending of troops, mechanical equipment and ammunition during the entire duration of
the work of the Council of the League of Nations and the work of the arbitration board ... The Italians
characterise us as a barbarous people whom it is necessary to civilise.

Haile Selassie's appeal to the democracies, 13 September 1935

Exercise 1

Document IV

Italy has her empire at last, a <u>Fascist empire</u> ... An empire of peace, because Italy desires peace, for herself and for all men, and she decides upon war only when it is forced upon her by imperious, 20 irrepressible necessities of life. An empire of civilisation and humanity for all the population of Abyssinia ...

The Italian people has created the empire with its blood. It will fertilise it with its labour.

Mussolini's speech on victory in Abyssinia, 9 May 1936

(a) In the context of these documents, what do you understand by:
(i) 'the Japanese fashion' (lines 1–2);
(ii) 'Geneva' (line 6); and
(iii) 'the Wal-Wal incident' (line 14)? (3)

(b) Explain the comment of 'Monsieur Laval' (line 6), 'If there were to be an exception it would no doubt be Moscow' (line 7). (3)

(c) In the context of Document IV, explain Mussolini's reference to 'a Fascist empire' (line 19). What characteristics of fascism are identifiable in this document? (4)

(d) In what way, and to what extent, does Document II corroborate the judgements of Mussolini on likely European reactions to the Abyssinian Crisis as given in Document I? (5)

(e) What is Haile Selassie's intention in these lines of his 'appeal' (Document III)? From the evidence of the language, content and tone of this document, how effective do you judge him to have been in presenting his argument? (4)

(f) Document I appears to offer a very different interpretation of Italian foreign policy at this time from that in Document IV. Identify and account for these differences. (6)

Exercise 2

Problems facing the Provisional Government – the Kornilov Revolt

document questions

Read the following documents from the prescribed texts and answer the questions which follow.

Document I

... on August 26 General Kornilov sent Vladimir Lvov, a member of the State Duma, with a demand for 1
the surrender by the Provisional Government of all civil and military power, so that he may form,
according to his wishes, a new government to administer the country. Deputy Lvov's authority to
make me such a proposal was confirmed subsequently by General Kornilov in his conversation with
me by direct wire. Realising that such demands, addressed to the Provisional Government through 5
me, revealed the longing of certain circles in Russian society to take advantage of the serious situation
the state finds itself in to set up a regime opposed to the gains of the revolution, the Provisional
Government finds it necessary to:

Authorise me, for the salvation of our motherland, of freedom and of our republican order, to
take prompt and decisive action to counter any attempt to limit Supreme Power in the state and 10
rights which the citizens have gained as a result of the revolution.

I am taking all necessary measures to protect the liberty and order of the country, and the
population will be informed in due course of the measures adopted.

A.F. Kerensky, Minister-President, Minister of War and the Navy, 27 August 1917

Document II

The first part of the Minister-President's telegram ... is a complete lie. It was not I who sent Vladimir
Lvov ... to the Provisional Government, but he came to me as the envoy of the Minister-President ... A 15
great provocation has thus taken place which puts the fate of the motherland in doubt.

People of Russia! Our great motherland is dying. The hour of her death is near. Obliged to speak
openly, I, General Kornilov, declare that under the pressure of the Bolshevik majority in the Soviets,
the Provisional Government is acting in complete accord with the plans of the German General
Staff, and simultaneously with the imminent landing of the enemy forces at Riga, it is destroying the 20
army and is undermining the very foundations of the country ...

I, General Kornilov, son of a Cossack peasant, declare to everyone that I want nothing for
myself, save the preservation of a Great Russia, and I swear that my goal for the people is the
convocation of a Constituent Assembly which will come about as a result of victory over the
enemy. 25

General Kornilov, 27 August 1917

Document III

Finally Kornilov came to the most important point ... He informed us that in the interests of maintaining order in the capital he had reached an agreement with Kerensky to move a large military force to Petrograd so that disturbances, if they occurred, could be suppressed immediately. It was quite clear from Kornilov's account that the Soviets ... were regarded as the main source of the possible disturbances and that by suppression of disturbances was understood the suppression of none other than the Soviets, and moreover that this was so understood not only in Stavka but also by Kerensky himself ... 30

In informing us of the agreement with Kerensky to send troops, he did not hide the fact that there were differences of opinion between them on the make up of the force and also on the appointment of a commander ... 35

There is no proof that Kornilov had a definite plan for using force not only against the Soviet, but against the legitimate government as well. Krymov's advance was directed against the Soviet.

Observations by a member of the Extraordinary Commission of Inquiry, N. Ukraintsev
(from *Novoye Russkoye Slovo*, published in New York, 28 October 1956)

(a) What is meant by (i) 'the Bolshevik majority in the Soviets' (line 18) and (ii) 'the convocation of a Constituent Assembly' (line 24)? (6)

(b) In what ways are Document I and Document II in conflict and to what extent are the differences resolved by Document III? (8)

(c) How useful are these documents in explaining the motives behind the actions and statements of Kerensky and of Kornilov? (8)

(d) What light do these extracts shed on the problems facing the Provisional Government in the summer and autumn of 1917? (8)

Exercise 3

Lenin and his opponents: the decision for revolution in October 1917

Read the following documents from the prescribed sources and answer the questions which follow.

Document I

The Bolsheviks, having obtained a majority in <u>the Soviets of Workers' and Soldiers' Deputies</u> of both 1
capitals, can and must take state power into their own hands.

They can do so because the active majority of revolutionary elements in the two chief cities is
large enough to carry the people with it, to overcome our opponents' resistance to smash them,
and to gain and retain power. For the Bolsheviks, by immediately proposing a democratic peace, 5
by immediately giving the land to the peasants and by re-establishing the democratic institutions
and liberties which have been distorted and shattered by Kerensky, will form a government which
nobody will be able to overthrow.

The majority of the people are on our side ... By seizing power both in Moscow and in
Petrograd at once (it doesn't matter which comes first, possibly Moscow), we shall win absolutely 10
and unquestionably.

Lenin in a letter, 12–14 September 1917

Document II

We are most profoundly convinced that to declare at once an armed uprising would mean to stake not
only the fate of our party, but also the fate of the Russian and <u>the international revolution</u> ... The
strength of our adversary is greater than it appears ... The strength of the proletarian party, of course,
is very considerable, but the decisive question is, is the mood among the workers and soldiers of the 15
capital really such, that they themselves see salvation already only in street fighting and are bursting
to go on to the streets? No. This mood does not exist ...

The party of the proletariat will grow, its programme will become clearer to even wider masses
... And there is only one way that it can nullify its successes in present circumstances, and that is
by taking the initiative for an uprising itself and in so doing subjecting the proletariat to the blows 20
of the whole united counter-revolution, supported by petit-bourgeois democracy.

We raise a warning voice against this ruinous policy.

Kamenev and Zinoviev, 11 October 1917

Exercise 3

- (a) Explain the references to (i) 'the Soviets of Workers' and Soldiers' Deputies' (line 1) and to (ii) 'the international revolution' (line 13). (8)

- (b) Consult Documents I and II. Why were Lenin's proposals opposed by his colleagues Kamenev and Zinoviev? (8)

- (c) Do Documents I and II provide convincing evidence of the extent of popular support enjoyed by the Bolsheviks by October 1917? (8)

- (d) How far does the evidence provided by Documents I and II explain the Bolsheviks' rise to power by October 1917? (9)

Exercise 4

Bolshevik rule in Russia

Study Documents I, II and III below and then answer questions (a) to (g) which follow.

Document I

In the tsar's day we organised thousands, and in Kerensky's hundreds of thousands. That is nothing 1
... That was preparatory work ... Until the vanguard of the workers learn to organise tens of
millions, they are not yet socialists and not creators of the socialist society, and will not acquire the
necessary experience of organisation ... The tasks of socialist construction demand persistent
prolonged work and corresponding experience, of which we have not enough. Even the next 5
immediately following generation, better developed than ours, will scarcely effect the full transition
to socialism.

(Lenin, writing c. 1918)

Document II

The peasant risings which formerly, before 1921, were ... a feature of the general Russian picture,
have almost completely disappeared. The peasantry is satisfied with the present position ... The
peasantry may be discontented with this or that ... That is of course possible and inevitable, since our 10
administrative machine and our state economy are still too defective to prevent that; but any serious
disaffection ... is ... completely excluded. This has been achieved in the course of a single year.

(Lenin, speaking in November 1922)

Document III

The seizure of control by a minority in Russia came as a grievous disappointment to American
democratic thought which had enthusiastically acclaimed the end of the tsars and the entrance of
Russia into the family of democratic nations. Subsequent events were even more disturbing. The right 15
of free speech and other civil liberties were denied. Even the advocacy of those rights which ...
constitute the foundation of freedom was declared to be counter-revolutionary and punishable by
death. Every form of political opposition was ruthlessly exterminated. There followed the deliberate
destruction of the economic life of the country. Attacks were made not only upon property in its so-
called capitalistic form, but recourse was had also to the requisitioning of labour. All voluntary 20
organisations of workers were brought to an end. To unionise or strike was followed by the severest
penalties. When labour retaliated by passive resistance, workmen were impressed into a huge labour
army. The practical effect of this programme was to plunge Russia once more into medievalism.
Politically there was a ruthless despotism and economically the situation was equally disastrous.

Exercise 4

It is true that, under pressure of the calamitous consequences, the governing group in Russia 25 has yielded certain concessions. The so-called new economic policy permitted a partial return to economic freedom ...

(Charles E. Hughes, US Secretary of State, writing in July 1923)

■ (a) What did Lenin mean when he wrote: 'In the tsar's day we organised thousands, and in Kerensky's hundreds of thousands' (line 1)? (2)

■ (b) Of what was Lenin warning in Document I, and how may he be said in this document to imply the need for dictatorship? (2)

■ (c) Show what Hughes meant by each of the following terms:
    (i) 'counter-revolutionary' (line 17);
    (ii) 'property in its so-called capitalistic form' (lines 19–20);
    (iii) 'the requisitioning of labour' (line 20). (3)

■ (d) 'the entrance of Russia into the family of democratic nations' (lines 14–15): when, and to what extent, was there justification for this judgement? (3)

■ (e) (i) With what recent change in Russia are Documents II and III both concerned?
    (ii) Why was this change made, and how far do you consider Lenin and Hughes each commented fittingly on the change? (5)

■ (f) How far do the language and style of Document III suggest that Hughes was a hostile witness concerning Bolshevik rule in Russia? (4)

■ (g) What characteristics of the rule of Lenin within Russia can be said to be illustrated in these documents? (6)

Exercise 5

Stalin's purges

Study Documents I, II, III and IV below and then answer questions (a) to (f) which follow.

Document I

It is clear that Stalinism is in the saddle and is determined ruthlessly to weed out Trotsky's doctrines 1
and supporters. But further aspects of the trial do little more than open up ... controversy. Why should
Stalin decide to deprive the USSR of the able – and in some cases almost indispensable – services of
such persons as ... Gregory Sokolnikov, who was credited with being chiefly responsible for Russia's
financial stability? ... Then again, why should Stalin take this step when Russia patently needs the 5
friendship of the democratic powers, as fascism marches strongly in Europe?

From *The New York Times*, March 1937

Document II

I know my hopelessness, faced by an infernal machine which ... fabricates slander. The NKVD ...
panders to Stalin's paranoia ... Any Central Committee member, any party member, can be ground to
dust by these monstrous organs and transformed into a traitor, a deviationist, a terrorist, a spy. If
Stalin doubts anyone, confirmation of his suspicions is instantaneous ... I was never a traitor. I would 10
have given my life for Lenin's life. I loved Kirov. I never plotted against Stalin.

From a secret letter written by Bukharin just before his execution in March 1938

Document III

Certain foreign pressmen have been talking drivel to the effect that the purging of Soviet organisations
of spies, assassins and wreckers like Trotsky, Zinoviev and other fiends has 'shaken' the Soviet
system and caused its 'demoralisation'. One can only laugh at such cheap drivel ... This Trotsky–
Bukharin bunch of spies, assassins and wreckers, who kow-towed to the foreign world, who were 15
possessed by a slavish instinct to grovel before every foreign bigwig, and who were ready to enter his
employ as a spy ... whom can they demoralise? ... Would it not be truer to say that the weeding out of
spies, assassins and wreckers from our Soviet organisations was bound to lead to the further
strengthening of these organisations?

Stalin, addressing a conference of Soviet Communist Party members, March 1939

Document IV

After Kirov's murder ... the political terror started. I caught only an occasional, accidental glimpse of 20
its inner workings ... In the late thirties Hitler was preparing his attack and doing everything he could
to undermine our military leadership. We helped him along by destroying the cream of our executive
personnel, our party leadership, and our scientific intelligentsia ... 1937 was the first year we didn't
fulfil <u>our Industrial Plan</u> ... But for years nobody raised a curtain on these facts ... In those days we still
had absolute faith in Stalin ... We thought we lacked Stalin's deep understanding of the political 25
struggle and were therefore unable to discern enemies in our midst in the way Stalin could.

From the autobiography of Nikita Khrushchev, prominent member of the Communist Party
during the 1930s and subsequently Soviet leader, written in the 1960s

(a) Explain what, in the context of these documents, you understand by each of the following:
(i) the 'NKVD' (line 7); and
(ii) 'our Industrial Plan' (line 24). (2)

(b) How does the explanation of the origin and purposes of Stalin's purges implied in Document II differ from that suggested in Document I? (3)

(c) What can be inferred from Documents II and III about the specific charges which were levelled against those who appeared as defendants in the 'show trials' of 1936–8? (5)

(d) Show how the language and arguments used in Document III might support the conclusion that Stalin was trying to exploit the nationalist instincts of his audience. (4)

(e) Document IV is an extract from an autobiography. Explain what reasons a historian might have for approaching this particular kind of source with caution, making reference, as appropriate, to the evidence of Document IV. (5)

(f) Using both the evidence of these documents and your own knowledge, discuss the nature and extent of the harm inflicted on the Soviet Union by Stalin's purges. (6)

Exercise 6

Support for the Nazis in the late 1920s and early 1930s

Study Documents I, II and III below and then answer questions (a) to (e) which follow.

Document I

During Hitler's struggle for power a large percentage of his followers were young people. Many young 1
Germans had been disappointed by the revolution of 1918 and the events that followed. They believed
that a thorough change in economic conditions was necessary, but the German democracy, even in its
Social-Democratic branch, was essentially conservative. In particular, lower middle-class idealists
who regarded Versailles as a national humiliation were prone to dream about a strong Reich ... and 5
Hitler seemed to offer this.

Another section of German youth followed Hitler because he promised a social revolution
which would at the same time be 'national'. They believed communism was 'Russian', 'cruel',
'unindividual' and 'anti-national'; they wanted a German revolution, a German socialism. Hitler
promised a future, jobs, recovery, a new national honour. And to those who supported him 10
actively by fighting in <u>the SA</u> he offered three marks a day, food, uniforms, and an adventurous
life.

The Nation, American newspaper, 27 June 1936

Document II

By their tremendous energy, by their strong emotions, by the novelty of their appeal, and in a period
of economic distress and national humiliation, the Nazis succeeded in rousing voters all over the
country, even in remote rural areas. Their campaigning combined immense exaltation with almost 15
bestial savagery.

The electorate was stirred. Radicalism combined with nationalism exercises a powerful
fascination on young voters who are bored by German party politics, take little interest in the
Reichstag, find the Socialists too dull and the Communists too sectarian and Russian, but have a
hatred of wealth and privilege, are themselves poor or menaced by poverty, and feel that 20
something is all wrong and that Jews, <u>the Young Plan</u>, the capitalists, the Stock Exchange, and
what not are responsible.

The New Statesman, British newspaper, 27 September 1930,
commenting on the results of the 1930 Reichstag elections

A-Level History: Europe of the Dictators, 1914–1945

155

Document III

The country is divided in an altogether unprecedented fashion. A minority composed of Hitlerites and Hugenberg Nationalists has been placed by the arbitrary decision of <u>the President</u> in supreme control of a majority which embraces practically all other parties ... The entire intelligentsia of the country ... 25 are, with very few exceptions, ranged against this minority. The Federation of German Industries, the Hansa League, representing the great shipping and export industries, the trades unions, the Episcopal and Catholic Churches, and what I might call moderate and reasonable people in all ranks are also ranged against a minority composed very largely of millions of immature young men and women on whose ignorance unscrupulous demagogues have successfully played. 30

Sir Horace Rumbold, British Ambassador to Germany, writing in February 1933

■ (a) (i) Identify 'the President' (line 24).
  (ii) What was 'the SA' (line 11)?
  (iii) What was 'the Young Plan' (line 21)? (3)

■ (b) How much similarity is there between the explanations offered in Documents I and II of the reasons why young German voters in the 1920s and early 1930s rejected:
  (i) the German Social Democratic Party; and
  (ii) the German Communist Party? (5)

■ (c) What do Documents I and II reveal of the positive attractions which Nazism had for the younger generation of German voters in the late 1920s and early 1930s? (6)

■ (d) In what ways do the language and tone of Document III suggest that its author was deeply hostile towards the Nazis? (4)

■ (e) In the light of their origins and content, explain the limitations of each of these documents as sources of information about the rise to power of the Nazis. (7)

Exercise 7

The Enabling Act

Read the following documents from the prescribed texts and answer the questions which follow.

Document I

The National Socialist movement will try to achieve its aim <u>with constitutional means</u> in this state. 1
The constitution prescribes only the methods, not the aim. In this constitutional way we shall try to
gain decisive majorities in the legislative bodies so that the moment we succeed we can <u>give the state
the form that corresponds to our ideas</u>.

    The chairman of the court summed up the statement to the effect that the setting up of the Third 5
Reich was being worked for in a constitutional way.

        Hitler, giving evidence at the trial of three army lieutenants accused of subversion in 1930

Document II

The Reich Chancellor opened the meeting and stated that ... he regarded the <u>events of 5 March</u> as
<u>revolution</u>. Ultimately Marxism would no longer exist in Germany. What was needed was an
Enabling Law passed by a two-thirds majority. He, the Reich Chancellor, was firmly convinced that
the Reichstag would pass such a law. The deputies of the German Communist Party would not appear 10
at the opening of the Reichstag because they were in jail ...

    He [Reich Minister Goering] stated that the two-thirds majority in the Reichstag would be
obtained for the Enabling Law. Deputies who left the session in order to make it impossible for the
two-thirds majority to be present would have to forfeit their free travel passes and allowances for
the duration of the legislative period. He wished to make a change in the rules to this effect. In his 15
opinion, the duty of the Deputy to exercise his mandate also entailed that he must not absent
himself from the sessions without being excused.

        Minutes of a Cabinet meeting held on 5 March 1933

Document III

But Hitler jumped up furiously and launched into a passionate reply. When the Social Democrats were
in power the National Socialists had been outlawed. Anyone who bowed down before an
International could not criticise the National Socialists. If the National Socialists had not a sense of 20
justice, the Social Democrats would not be here in the hall. But the National Socialists had resisted the
temptation to turn against those who had tormented them for fourteen years. 'You are oversensitive,
gentlemen, if you talk of persecution already. By God, the National Socialists would have had the
courage to deal with the Social Democrats in a different way ... You, gentlemen, are no longer needed.

I do not even want you to vote for the Enabling Act. Germany shall become free, but not through you.' 25
... We tried to dam the flood of Hitler's unjust accusations with interruptions of 'No!', 'An error!', 'False!' But that did us no good. The SA and SS people, who surrounded us in a semicircle along the walls of the hall, hissed loudly and murmured: 'Shut up!', 'Traitors!', 'You'll be strung up today.'

> An account by a Bavarian SPD deputy of the debate in the
> Reichstag on the Enabling Act, 24 March 1933

(a) What did Hitler mean by saying that the National Socialist movement would try to achieve its aim 'with constitutional means' (line 1)? (4)

(b) Explain why Hitler should have regarded the 'events of 5 March' as a 'revolution' (lines 7–8). (4)

(c) In the light of Documents I and II, how far did Hitler abide by the pledge he had made in Document I? (6)

(d) How far do Documents I and III help to explain the ease with which the Enabling Act was passed? (8)

(e) How did Hitler use the Enabling Act in 1933 to 'give the state the form that corresponds to our ideas' (lines 3–4)? (8)

Exercise 8

'The Night of the Long Knives' and its consequences

Study Documents I, II and III below and then answer questions (a) to (f) which follow.

Document I

We are still in the dark about the grisly events of 30 June. We know only that men whom Hitler had 1
lauded to the skies are dead, and by his act. We are told they are dead because they were engaged in a
conspiracy which, had it matured, would have meant civil war. And of course we are invited to
admire the courageous decisiveness of the Führer who rids himself of rivals without trial or evidence.
But so far not a scrap of evidence has been produced to prove a conspiracy ...   5

    The whole thing bears all the marks of tyranny. Men without any serious principles were able
to seize power ... Hitler hears mutterings of discontent; he begins to get nerves; like a weak bully
he conceives murder upon the basis of conspiracy to be the way out. The discontent becomes, for
publicity purposes, a gigantic conspiracy. It is a well-known device of all tyrants to execute on
suspicion before discontent is in a position to utter challenge.   10

Harold Laski, British author, writing in *The Daily Herald*, July 1934

Document II

It is of course extremely difficult for Sir Eric Phipps ... to form a definite judgement as to the real cause
which brought about the murders on June 30. But I confess the picture he draws has not shaken my
disbelief in the existence of a Schleicher–Röhm plot. That there was a great and growing divergence of
views and policy between Hitler and Röhm, between the SA and the army, and between the left wing
and the right wing, is obvious, and it was equally obvious that Hitler sooner or later would have to 15
come down on one side or the other. But this despatch supplies no evidence whatever to show that the
purge ... was precipitated by the decision of Röhm and Schleicher to launch a *coup d'état*.

    From the point of view of practical politics the matter is of no particular importance. What is
important is that the upshot of the whole matter is the emergence of the army as the dominant
force in Germany today.   20

O. G. Sargent, British diplomat, commenting on a despatch from Sir Eric Phipps,
British Ambassador to Germany, July 1934

Exercise 8

Document III

Röhm was considered as a man on the left wing of the party and one of those who believed that a second more radical revolution was necessary. His elimination therefore while primarily a stern lesson in party discipline would seem to indicate a temporary dissolution of the strength of the radicals and to that extent increased strength to the conservative elements which desire a more liberal domestic and foreign policy with eventual monarchist leanings.

25

W. E. Dodd, American Ambassador to Germany, reporting to US Secretary of State, July 1934

(a) Identify (i) 'Röhm' (lines 13, 14, 17 and 21) and (ii) 'the SA' (line 14).   (2)

(b) What can be inferred from these documents concerning Röhm's stance and sympathies in the internal politics of the Nazi Party in 1933–4?   (3)

(c) (i) What indications are there in Documents I and II of the explanation which Hitler offered in public for the events of 30 June 1934?
    (ii) To what extent is this explanation accepted by the authors of Documents I and II?   (5)

(d) Explain, and account for, the difference in language and tone between Document I on the one hand and Documents II and III on the other.   (4)

(e) Note the origin of each of these documents. In the light of their origins, discuss their value to a historian of events in Germany in 1934.   (4)

(f) To what extent are the authors of Documents II and III in agreement regarding the likely political consequences within Germany of Hitler's purge of 30 June 1934? How far were these predictions justified in the event?   (7)

Exercise 9

Economic problems in the Third Reich

Read the following documents from the prescribed texts and answer the questions which follow.

Document I

It is assumed under the <u>New Plan</u> that, in view of the decline in German exports and the consequent 1
decline in foreign exchange receipts, the issue of foreign currency permits will be to a large degree
restricted to vital foodstuffs as well as to raw materials and semi-manufactured goods. Even here
considerable restrictions will have to be imposed. Outside the foreign exchange plan the system of
barter transactions will be expanded. As regards essential commodities, barter transactions will be 5
sanctioned provided that they do not require foreign exchange. In the case of non-essential
commodities, an effort must be made to obtain foreign exchange through barter transactions too, for
example by exporting more goods from Germany than are imported.

... Treaty arrangements will not be infringed. The import of goods in itself can continue in the
same way as hitherto, but the German importer who concludes transactions and imports goods 10
without previously receiving a foreign currency permit will be aware from the outset that he
cannot count on an allocation of foreign exchange.

Dr Karl Ritter, Director of Economics Department in the Foreign Office, September 1934

Document II

One of the most important tasks of the <u>German Labour Front</u> is vocational training. Vocational
training is not only a priority in view of the <u>Four-Year Plan</u> in order to make every working citizen into
as valuable a worker for the nation as possible; it is also important for the individual ... It is well 15
known that the German worker in particular has always felt a deep need to continue his studies
because he has felt that he could only improve his social position by new achievements. In addition
there is the current shortage of skilled workers. The <u>German Labour Front</u> has done, and is still doing,
almost everything possible to alleviate this shortage. The establishment of training centres, the
construction of training shops, the additional training of engineers and technicians, a comprehensive 20
specialist press, the encouragement of technical colleges – these are the methods which the <u>German
Labour Front</u> has adopted in the sphere of vocational training.

Extract from an official publication of the German Labour Front

Exercise 9

(a) Why was the New Plan, referred to in Document I, introduced? (6)

(b) What was the German Labour Front, referred to in Document II, and how was it organised? (6)

(c) How important are these documents in illustrating a change in Nazi economic focus? (6)

(d) How successful was the Four-Year Plan by 1939? (6)

(e) What light do these documents shed on the economic problems facing the Third Reich? (6)

Exercise 10

The Hossbach Memorandum

Read the following documents from the prescribed texts and answer the questions which follow.

Document I

His exposition to follow was the fruit of thorough deliberation and the experiences of his four-and-a-half years of power. He wished to explain to the gentlemen present his basic ideas concerning the opportunities for the development of our position in the field of foreign affairs and its requirements, and he asked, in the interest of a long-term German policy, that his exposition be regarded, in the event of his death, as his last will and testament ...   5

The aim of German policy was to make secure and to preserve the racial community ... and to enlarge it. It was therefore a question of space.

Hitler, from the Hossbach Memorandum of a meeting in the Reich Chancellery, 5 November 1937

Document II

When Germany has achieved complete preparedness for war in all spheres, then the military conditions will have been created for carrying out an offensive war against Czechoslovakia, so that the solution of the German problem of living space can be carried to a victorious conclusion even if   10 one or another of the Great Powers intervene against us ...

Should the political situation not develop, or develop only slowly, in our favour, then the execution of 'Operation Green' from our side will have to be postponed for years. If, however, a situation arises which, owing to Britain's aversion to a general European War, through her lack of interest in the Central European problem and because of a conflict breaking out between Italy and   15 France in the Mediterranean, creates the probability that Germany will face no other opponent than Russia on Czechoslovakia's side, then 'Operation Green' will start before the completion of Germany's full preparedness for war.

Memorandum by General Jodl, Chief of Operations Staff at OKW, 7 December 1937

  ■ (a) Explain the meaning of 'racial community' in line 6, and 'the German problem of living space' in line 10. (6)

  ■ (b) Why was the meeting referred to in Document I called by Hitler? (6)

  ■ (c) In what ways does Document II modify the plans outlined in the Hossbach Memorandum? (6)

  ■ (d) How useful are these passages as an explanation of Hitler's policy in eastern Europe? (6)

  ■ (e) Why has the Hossbach Memorandum aroused such controversy amongst historians? (6)

Exercise 1

The Abyssinian Crisis

■ (a) (i) 'The Japanese fashion' refers to the 'Manchurian Incident' of 18 September 1931, when Japanese troops occupied Manchuria very swiftly and without a declaration of war, on the excuse that Chinese soldiers had blown up some three feet of railway line at Mukden.

(ii) 'Geneva' here means the League of Nations, whose headquarters were in Geneva. The League would certainly follow the lead of France and Britain in dealing with Abyssinia because they were the only two countries able to put direct pressure on Italy.

(iii) 'The Wal-Wal incident' (December 1934) provided Mussolini with an excuse to launch the invasion of Abyssinia. A skirmish between Italian and Abyssinian troops took place at the oasis of Wal-Wal in which thirty Italian soldiers were killed. The League set up an inquiry, but Mussolini had already planned the invasion which began in October 1935.

*Although only one mark is given for each answer, remember that scoring full marks in such a question represents three marks out of a total of twenty-five; you would find it difficult to earn 3/25 in an essay question for writing six sentences! Remember also that it's usually easier to score marks in **document questions** than in **essay questions**, not least because it's easier to gain full marks on any section, whereas it's very difficult to score anything like full marks on an essay question.*

*So, although you should never waste valuable time in writing too much on this type of **definition question** (the marks allotted should warn you against that) you must note that the words or phrases have to be defined '**in the context of these documents**' and this makes it unlikely that one-word definitions will gain you full marks. Two sentences would be about the average, as is the case here; each part of the question is defined in terms of the period to which the document in question belongs.*

■ (b) Pierre Laval, the French Foreign Minister, and Sir Samuel Hoare, British Foreign Secretary, met in December 1935, to draw up a scheme 'giving Italy territorial concessions and guaranteed influence [in Ethiopia] but maintaining an independent Ethiopian state' (Overy). Both Britain and France were willing to give Italy something in Ethiopia, if she did not ally with Hitler's Germany. In the Soviet Union, a new policy of 'qualified support for the western strategy of collective security' was adopted in 1934. The Soviet Union joined the League in September, but she was soon disillusioned by Britain and France who wished to reach agreement with Italy. Laval's comment shows him to be well aware of the Soviet Union's likely attitude.

■ (c) Mussolini's fascist empire, as described in this document, reveals many of the contradictions of fascism. It was hardly 'an empire of peace' when it had been conquered in a bloody and one-sided war; that war had not been forced upon Italy but was the climax of a deliberate decision to expand into Africa; now the Abyssinians faced a future which was the very opposite of civilised and humane. Fascist propaganda is exemplified by these contradictions: the claim that Italy desires peace, while the reference to the creation of an empire with the blood of Italians and its fertilisation with their labour is more in keeping with Mussolini's love of war; the grandiose schemes of public works for which he is still remembered in Italy; and his doomed attempt to make Italians a more warlike people.

Double questions are just as likely to be asked about documents as they are to appear in essay questions. As always, the question of balance is important; although the total marks for the question are provided, there's no indication as to their allocation within the question. So you've got to decide how many marks will be allocated to each part.

Exercise 1

(d) In Document I, Mussolini stresses the need for a quick and decisive war against Abyssinia and for a declaration to 'England and France that their interests would be recognised'. By January, after the attack had become bogged down, Laval wishes Mussolini to have 'at least part of the territory he has conquered'; Hoare agrees that Abyssinia should cede territory in the north, but cautions that aggression must not be rewarded or the League will be blamed. Thus Mussolini was right in claiming in Document I that the western powers would not prevent his aggression, but was wrong in assuming that they would agree to his taking the whole of Abyssinia – in the end the public outcry in Britain caused Parliament to reject the Hoare–Laval agreement and Mussolini was left facing the hostility of Britain, France and the League.

(e) This 'appeal to the democracies' was made after the League's arbitration board had reported that neither side was at fault in the Wal-Wal incident (3 September 1935) and before the Italian invasion began on 2 October 1935. Selassie intends to show that Italian preparations for war had begun 'five months' before the fighting at Wal-Wal and had since intensified. Lines 17–18 indicate that he foresaw the coming invasion and quotes an Italian justification for it. He provides some detailed evidence of these charges ('troops, mechanised equipment and ammunition') and appeals for the sympathy of the democracies, but this could not be effective given the views of Britain and France as expressed in Document II.

(f) Document I provides a typically cynical diplomatic view of the necessity for a speedy war of conquest, written nine months before the invasion took place and after the Wal-Wal incident. There must be no declaration of war, 'we must always emphasise the purely defensive character of operations' and 'no one in Europe would raise any difficulties'. In Document IV, a public speech, Mussolini would provide a very different explanation of Italian policy. The peaceful intentions and civilising mission of Italy are both stressed (lines 19–20) and the Italian people will fertilise a supposedly barren region with its labour. In May 1936, Mussolini needs to find the most convincing reasons that he can to justify a lengthy war, won by a massive and ruinously expensive war effort, which had incurred the hostility of Britain, France and the League and begun that sequence of events which was to thrust Italy into her fatal alliance with Germany.

Exercise 2

Problems facing the Provisional Government – the Kornilov Revolt

■ (a) (i) Soviets, particularly the most important in Petrograd, had been set up after the February Revolution. By the end of August it was clear that the Bolsheviks commanded a majority in the Petrograd Soviet; during September, they obtained majorities in the Moscow Soviet and elsewhere. Kornilov and the right saw the Soviets as the chief danger to the state.

(ii) The creation of a democratically elected Constituent Assembly had been the goal of Russian liberals since 1905. After the February Revolution, the Provisional Government was working towards the election of a Constituent Assembly, while the Bolsheviks, knowing that they could not hope for a majority in such a body, preferred to call for 'All power to the Soviets'.

*At first sight this looks like a **definition question**, but the marks given for it show that a longer answer is required. How long that answer is to be will depend on the number of marks allotted to the question and the overall length of the answers to a document question.*

*Some examining boards will help you to find passages referred to in questions by underlining, etc. You should make use of this yourself when looking for answers as you read through the documents: you should **underline** (possibly using different colours) the words or phrases which you'll use in your answer. '**Highlighter**' pens may also be used, but it may be best to keep these for the answers to one question only, probably the last.*

■ (b) Documents I and II conflict first over the part played in negotiations by Vladimir Lvov. Kerensky claims that he was sent by Kornilov with a demand for the Provisional Government to surrender its power (lines 1–2); Kornilov claims that Lvov was sent to him as 'the envoy of the Minister-President'. Document III does not touch on this aspect, but it appears that Lvov misrepresented himself as an emissary with authority to speak for Kerensky when he visited Kornilov at Mogilev (25 August 1917).

More importantly, Kerensky claims, in Document I, that Kornilov's message declared that he (Kornilov) would form 'according to his wishes, a new government to administer the country'. Such a regime would be 'opposed to the gains of the revolution' and would be backed by 'certain circles in Russian society' who wished to take advantage of the military crisis (lines 6–7). Kornilov, in Document II, also sees a crisis ('our great motherland is dying') but declares that the Provisional Government is in league with the German General Staff and under pressure from the 'Bolshevik majority in the Soviets'. Kornilov states that he only wishes to bring about 'the convocation of a Constituent Assembly' which does not imply that he is an opponent of the revolution.

Document III finds that Kornilov claims an agreement with Kerensky 'to move a large military force to Petrograd' with the Soviet as its main target (lines 27–8). But there is no proof that this force was destined to be used against the 'legitimate government as well'.

Thus Document III acquits Kornilov of treason against the Provisional Government as charged by Kerensky in Document I, but is silent on Kornilov's charges of treasonable activities by the Provisional Government (lines 17–21).

Exercise 2

■ **(c)** Document I sees Kerensky seeking to provide justification for the emergency measures he wishes to take against the Kornilov threat. Document III declares that threat to be exaggerated (lines 36–7) as does Kornilov's statement (lines 22–5). Kerensky was prone to vacillation and recent research indicates that, although he supported Kornilov's desire for measures to restore military discipline, he feared resistance from the Petrograd Soviet. When he received Lvov's report on Kornilov's wish for a military dictatorship, he concluded that there was a conspiracy against him.

Kornilov's statement of his motives (lines 22–5) is a rhetorical justification for his stand and must be treated with suspicion. He says nothing of defending the revolution, only supporting a Constituent Assembly which might well have produced a government more in line with the desires of the right, of which he was an obvious supporter. His chief concern appears to be the restoration of the Russian nation by military victory.

Document III deals only with Kornilov and his motives; it is generally sympathetic towards him. The Commission was much impressed with a tape which recorded discussions between Kornilov and Kerensky and also by its failure to obtain satisfactory answers when interviewing the latter.

■ **(d)** These documents show the problems facing the Provisional Government as (1) the existence of 'certain circles in Russian society' who wish to 'set up a regime opposed to the gains of the revolution'; (2) the critical military situation threatening Petrograd ('the imminent landing of the enemy forces at Riga'); (3) the danger to the Provisional Government of a hostile 'Bolshevik majority in the Soviets' which might cause 'disturbances' in the capital.

Much of this concerns the Provisional Government's lack of legitimacy, its doomed attempts to govern under the 'Dual Power' system, and its lack of authority without the backing of the police or the Cossacks and with an army which was dangerously unreliable. Lenin had forced the government to face the problems of 'Peace, Bread and Land': the failure to give land to the peasants was suicidal;

similarly 'the government failed to cater for the [economic] needs of the workers and paid the political price' (Acton); most important of all was the failure to end the war.

These extracts do not confront the underlying problems of the Provisional Government, but they do sum up the immediate difficulties faced in the summer and autumn of 1917.

Lenin and his opponents – the decision for revolution in October 1917

■ (a) (i) 'The Soviet of Workers' and Soldiers' Deputies' was established (27 February 1917), at the climax of the February Revolution. It shared power with the Provisional Government (in the so-called 'Dual Power' system) and was under moderate socialist control until September 1917. The Bolsheviks obtained majorities in the Petrograd and Moscow Soviets in September and revived their call for 'All power to the Soviets'. Lenin now claimed that the Bolsheviks were in a position to take power themselves.

(ii) The Bolshevik Party and its leaders were dedicated to the cause of international revolution. For them, revolution in Russia would be only a part of this revolution. Kamenev and Zinoviev, in stressing the danger of premature armed uprising, were naturally also stressing the effects of failure on the international revolution as well as on the Bolshevik Party and the Russian revolution – and this argument would appeal to the Central Committee.

Where the questions are being set on prescribed sources, they'll be more difficult and require a more detailed knowledge of the topic. **Questions (c) and (d)** *both require answers based on a comparison between what is said in the documents and what you already know; in* **Question (b)** *the answer is to be found in the documents, although it would be improved by some mention of the real reasons for the position taken by both sides.*

■ (b) Lenin's proposals were that the party 'can and must take state power into their own hands ... by seizing power both in Moscow and in Petrograd at once'. Kamenev and Zinoviev opposed an uprising because 'the strength of our adversary is greater than it appears' and because they doubted whether, at this time, 'the workers and soldiers of the capital ... see salvation only in street fighting and are bursting to go on the streets'. They claim that the party will grow as its message becomes clear to more people (lines 18–19) and they warn that the only danger it faces is to take 'the initiative for an uprising itself', thus 'subjecting the proletariat to the blows of the whole united counter-revolution, supported by petit-bourgeois democracy'.

Thus these two members of the Central Committee (the only two who dissented from the vital vote on 10 October, and made their protest the next day) denied that the majority of people were 'already for us' and equally that the 'majority of the international proletariat' felt the same way. To them, immediate revolution was a 'ruinous policy'; they wanted a revolution at a later date.

These documents provide a clear answer to the question, but don't reveal what the true motives on both sides might have been. **Orlando Figes**, *in his* A People's Tragedy, *shows that Lenin's insistence on an immediate revolution sprang not only from the fear that Kerensky would 'organise repressive measures against it' (this reason that he gave for immediate revolution was obvious nonsense: 'Kerensky was quite incapable of such decisive action and ... the government was powerless to put any counter-revolutionary intentions into practice') but more from the belief that power must be seized by the Bolsheviks before the Soviet Congress met. If not, he would have* *reasoned, a coalition government with at least the left wing of the SRs and Mensheviks would be formed and 'Kamenev, Lenin's arch rival in the Bolshevik Party ... would no doubt emerge as the central figure in such a coalition'. Thus Lenin ran the risk of being side-lined, even refused office, if this should happen; the only way in which the Bolsheviks, with Lenin in command, could emerge as masters of the situation would be by taking power before the Congress met.*

Such an explanation explains both Lenin's insistence on haste and would give added reason for Kamenev and Zinoviev to urge that the obvious strategy was to wait for the 'forthcoming Congress [which] would almost certainly endorse the Bolshevik call for a transfer of power to the Soviets'.

(c) In Document I, Lenin states that the Bolsheviks have a majority in the Soviets of 'both capitals' (lines 1–2). He claims that 'the active majority of revolutionary elements in the two cities is large enough to carry the people with it' and together they can overcome resistance and 'gain and retain power' – thus he alleges that 'the majority of people are on our side'.

In Document II, his opponents admit that 'the strength of the proletarian party ... is very considerable' but refuse to believe that 'the mood among the workers and soldiers of the capital' indicates that they are 'bursting to go on the streets'.

By Lenin's argument, the majorities obtained during September and October in the Soviets of Petrograd, Moscow and elsewhere showed support for their slogans (lines 5–8) but did not indicate that workers and soldiers were ready to take to the streets to put the Bolsheviks in power. His faith in the ability of the party to 'carry the people' with them is similarly unsupported by evidence. The conclusion that 'the majority of people are on our side' appears optimistic and unproven.

His opponents were probably more accurate in doubting 'the mood among the workers and soldiers'; in the event, 'the leadership undertook extensive soundings with lower-party bodies' which revealed overwhelming support for 'a transfer of power to the Soviets' but also 'a widespread reluctance to "come out"' (Acton), particularly in the name of the Bolshevik Party.

*This answer to **Question (c)** summarises the evidence given in the documents for popular support for the Bolsheviks and adds, in the last paragraph, a modern historian's view of the strength of such support. More could be made of this, in view of the necessity of deciding whether the documentary evidence is 'convincing'.*

(d) In Document I, the Bolshevik success appears to come from their majorities in the Soviets, the power of the party 'to carry the people with it', the popularity of their slogans (lines 5–8) and the eventual seizure of power in Petrograd and Moscow.

In Document II, the 'ruinous policy' was not, in the end, ruinous at all, but the success of the Bolsheviks in October came from the vital adaptation by the Central Committee and Trotsky of the tactics proposed by Lenin, using the Petrograd Soviet rather than the party to overthrow Kerensky. The seizure of power by the party was integrated with moves by the Soviet to defend the capital against the feared attack from the Germans and any assault on the left by the government. Through the Soviet's Military Revolutionary Committee (MRC), with its Bolshevik majority, Trotsky was able to combine the determination of the Soviet to prevent a *coup* against the left by the Provisional Government with the Bolshevik determination to bring down that government and take its place.

Thus Lenin was right to see the importance of Bolshevik control of the Soviets and the need for immediate armed insurrection, but wrong in seeing the party, rather than the Soviets, as the means by which victory might be obtained.

Again, the claims for the Bolshevik Party, put forward by Lenin in **Document I**, *are contrasted with the actual means by which the October Revolution succeeded.*

Bolshevik rule in Russia

■ **(a)** Lenin was referring to the size of the Bolshevik Party (a) before the February Revolution of 1917 and (b) during the rule of the Provisional Government, ultimately under Kerensky's leadership. Lenin had always insisted that to obtain power the party should be, in Trotsky's words, 'an exclusive, tight-structured, professional organisation'.

*Here we have more questions than usual and it's very important **(a)** to pay careful attention to the number of marks available for each question and **(b)** to resist the temptation to write too much on any one answer. As a very general rule, you can assume that one mark is given for each important fact in an answer. Thus, in **Question (a)**, to which two marks are allocated, there must be something more required than a simple explanation of Lenin's phrase; I've tried to provide it in the second sentence of my answer. Perhaps it needs a little more explanation; do you think so?*

■ **(b)** Lenin states what the creation of a socialist society needs (lines 2–4). He knows that 'the full transition to socialism' may not occur even in 'the next immediately following generation'. The need for dictatorship is implied in the phrase 'until the vanguard of the workers learn to organise tens of millions' – i.e. control of the people by a dictatorship of the 'vanguard of the workers', that is to say, the Bolshevik Party.

*The answer to the first part of **Question (b)** could be improved by the substitution of the word* **'warns'** *for* **'knows'** *in the second sentence. Always try to introduce* **key words** *in the question into your answer; it shows the reader that you're trying to answer the question and may remind you what the question actually is.*

■ **(c)** **(i)** 'Counter-revolutionary' is an adjective which was applied to any action which appeared to oppose the revolution. Any action by an opponent could be labelled counter-revolutionary by the Cheka during the Terror which followed the October Revolution.

(ii) This refers to the seizure of property by the Bolshevik state under the Decrees of 'Land' and 'Workers' Control' (both November 1917). The estates of landowners and the factories of businessmen were confiscated under these decrees during the period of 'state capitalism' (November 1917 to June 1918). Hughes, writing in 1923, would also have been familiar with the more stringent Decree of Nationalisation and the 'requisitioning squads' which were both a feature of War Communism (1918–21).

(iii) War Communism involved the nationalisation of almost all industry, and the consequent control over labour by the central government. With the end of trade union power (lines 20–2), 'workmen were impressed into a huge labour army'.

*Question **(c)**, worth only three marks in total, has probably too long an answer here. In other words, I've fallen into the trap I warned you against above. Now, how would you cut down these answers, particularly* **(c)(ii)**?

■ **(d)** Hughes here states that, with the advent of the Provisional Government after the February Revolution, Russia had entered 'the family of democratic nations'. Considering that the Provisional Government was both provisional and unelected, and that the first elected Constituent Assembly did not meet until the Provisional Government had been deposed in the October Revolution (and was then dissolved after one day's session) it is obviously premature to claim that Russia was a democracy between February and October 1917. Nor was this true during the period of Bolshevik rule under Lenin: he later confessed to Trotsky that the dissolution of the Constituent Assembly 'means a complete and frank liquidation of the idea of democracy by the idea of dictatorship'.

> **Question (d)** *seems to represent a good three marks worth of answer; it implies, but does not claim, that Russia never 'entered the family of democratic nations' after the February Revolution. If you find your answer implying something strongly, don't be afraid to spell it out!*

■ **(e)** **(i)** Both these documents are concerned with the introduction of the New Economic Policy (NEP) in March 1921.

(ii) The introduction of the NEP resulted from the crisis of 1921, itself brought about by the failures of War Communism: a drastic fall in industrial output, one in five of the population starving, growing opposition within the party and a threat to Bolshevik rule by strikes in industry and virtual guerrilla war in the countryside, culminating in the Kronstadt revolt.

Lenin was correct in stating that the abolition of grain requisitioning had put an end to the dangerous peasant risings of 1921. But it was not true to say that 'any serious disaffection … is … completely excluded'; the NEP failed to solve the endemic problems of Soviet agriculture. Hughes correctly sees 'a partial return to economic freedom' in the NEP, but implies that it was not certain to last.

> **Question (e)** *provides an excellent example of the importance of clear thinking about the mark allocation before you begin to write. Looking at the question, you can immediately see* **four** *clear parts which require individual answers which would be worth at least* **one mark***. Which answer will be worth* **two marks***? I've assumed it's 'Why was this change made…?' and drawn attention to that fact by giving it a separate paragraph and a longer answer than the others.*

■ **(f)** The exaggerated tone of Document III shows the disapproval felt by Hughes for the development of Bolshevik rule. The 'grievous disappointment to American democratic thought' was followed by 'even more disturbing' events, including the 'destruction of the economic life of the country' which 'was to plunge Russia once more into medievalism'. The phrases that he uses show no sympathy for the minority who had seized control: political opposition was 'ruthlessly exterminated', the political system was a 'ruthless despotism' and the 'so-called new economic policy' permitted no more than a 'partial return to economic freedom'. Perhaps no other reaction could be expected from a member of a Republican administration in 1923.

■ **(g)** Document I stresses the new and enlarged role for the Bolshevik Party after a successful revolution, together with Lenin's belief that the building of a socialist society would be a lengthy process. Document II illustrates the continuing problem of the place of the peasantry in a society primarily organised for the benefit of the industrial proletariat. Lenin always regarded the NEP as a retreat, if only a temporary one; it was left to Stalin to solve the problem by collectivisation imposed by force. Document III draws attention to the 'ruthless despotism', brooking no opposition, of Lenin's state; Acton has shown how an 'essentially popular revolution' was rapidly turned into a ... one-party dictatorship' dependent on a policy of terror. The economic life of the country was similarly controlled in the era of War Communism until the reluctant appearance of the NEP which provided 'a partial return to economic freedom', unmatched by any loosening of political control.

Stalin's purges

■ **(a)** **(i)** The NKVD denoted the Soviet secret police, under the leadership of Yagoda, which had superseded the OGPU in 1934. The Decree Against Terrorist Acts, issued after Kirov's murder, 'made the NKVD a law unto itself in the pursuit of enemies of the state and of the Party' (Lynch).

(ii) This refers to the Second Four-Year Plan (1933–7). Alec Nove notes 'a grave shortage of qualified personnel' at this time; widespread charges of 'sabotage' had a detrimental effect on industrial productivity.

> *One mark for each answer in* **Question (a)** *shows a straightforward* **definition question**. *The second sentence in each of my answers may be taken as* '**insurance**'*: both are relevant to the question but the simple definition of the first sentences might have been enough to gain a mark for each.*

■ **(b)** In Document II, Bukharin sees the origin of the purges in 'Stalin's paranoia'. In Document I, the origins are found in the determination of Stalinism 'ruthlessly to weed out Trotsky's doctrines and supporters'. Bukharin finds no purpose in the purges, beyond Stalin's suspicions of everyone's loyalty; *The New York Times* stresses the absurdity of an anti-Trotsky policy which deprives 'the USSR of the able ... services of such persons as ... Gregory Sokolnikov' and 'the friendship of the democratic powers'.

> *Note how the words* '**origins**' *and* '**purpose**' *are included in the answer to echo their use in the question. Don't spend valuable time trying to work out where the third mark will be given; in this case, it may not be allocated to one particular part of the question.*

■ **(c)** In Document II, Bukharin finds that anyone – 'any Central Committee member, any party member' – can be transformed by the slander of the NKVD into 'a traitor, a deviationist, a terrorist, a spy'. In Document III, Stalin speaks of 'spies, assassins and wreckers' who 'kow-towed to the foreign world' and were ready to spy for foreign countries. The charges at the 'show trials' thus covered all types of opposition to the regime: those who deviated from the party line like Trotsky; those who 'spied' for foreign countries, thus feeding the suspicion of foreigners felt by most Russians or 'wrecked' production in the factories (and provided an excellent excuse for missing targets in the Four-Year Plans); and those who could be blamed for such mysterious deaths as that of Kirov. Ultimately, of course, the actual charges were of little importance as the accused could be made to admit to almost any crime.

> *You must be clear about the difference between* '**infer**' *and* '**imply**'. *The last sentence provides an important point which is not immediately obvious when you start thinking about your answer.*

■ **(d)** Stalin was on firm ground in attacking foreigners in Document III: most Soviet communists were pathologically suspicious of their activities. The language is emotive: references to 'fiends ... cheap drivel ... this Trotsky–Bukharin bunch of spies, assassins and wreckers ... kow-towed ... a slavish instinct to grovel before every foreign bigwig'. The expressions are slangy, to appeal to his audience of party workers, and full of hatred for foreigners to appeal to instincts of nationalism. The statement that 'our Soviet organisations' would be strengthened rather than demoralised by the 'weeding out of spies, assassins and wreckers' was one of the few arguments which might begin to explain the vast numbers removed in the purges – the appeal to nationalist sentiment was a necessary strengthening of that argument.

With reference to the argument in the last sentence of this answer, it could be worth stressing that the more spies, assassins and wreckers who could be weeded out, the more they might be replaced by members of his audience. Always read the information given about the origins of the documents with great care; they'll often provide some, occasionally all, of the required answer.

(e) Historians need to approach autobiographies with caution because their authors are normally seeking to enhance their reputation by excusing their mistakes and exaggerating their successes. Time may have distorted their memories, but they can also be selective in their use of evidence, producing half-truths and lies whenever it is difficult to contradict them. Khrushchev's statement (lines 23–4) when writing of the 'political terror' seems very unlikely for a man who was Secretary of the Moscow District Party Committee (1934–8) and General Secretary of the Ukraine thereafter. No evidence is offered for the claim that Hitler was undermining Soviet military leadership, although the following sentence is certainly true – a point that could be safely made in the 1960s. The final excuse (lines 25–6) seems unlikely to be true for a period in which prominent members of the party were primarily engaged in avoiding being purged themselves.

*In **Question (e)**, note what is said about the weakness of **autobiographies** as evidence. This is the sort of information which you need to put down, almost without thinking, before you go on to give the specific instances normally required by the question. You don't want to be groping around for things to say about autobiographies in the midst of an exam; learn them, and the criticisms of other types of evidence, during your revision. And don't forget to note the date when the autobiography was written: it may tell you quite a lot about its worth.*

(f) The extent of Stalin's purges has been much debated and variously assessed, but the total certainly runs into millions. As Khrushchev points out, 'the cream of our executive personnel, our party leadership, and our scientific intelligentsia' were destroyed – he might have added that the 'gigantic conspiracy' announced by Vyshinsky in May 1937 was to cost the Red Army its Chief-of-Staff, three of the five Marshals of the Soviet Union, fourteen of the sixteen army commanders and half of the commissioned officers either imprisoned or shot. Important individuals such as Sokolnikov (line 4) were removed; Bukharin states (lines 9–11) that no-one was safe; Stalin had to counter foreign charges of 'demoralisation' in the Soviet system (lines 14–17); Khrushchev admits that '1937 was the first year we didn't fulfil our Industrial Plan'. Above all, 'for the totality of the population 1936–8 was a nightmare' (Hosking) in which none could feel safe from arrest.

*The answer to **Question (f)** is on the short side for one that is worth six marks, but it seems to contain enough facts, both from the documents and from 'your own knowledge', to get most of those marks. It could be improved by being written in two paragraphs – one taken from the documents, one from 'your own knowledge' – and perhaps by being expanded a little.*

Support for the Nazis in the late 1920s and early 1930s

■ (a) (i) The President is Paul von Hindenburg, President of the Weimar Republic, 1925–34.

(ii) The SA (Stormtroopers) were the paramilitary organisation of the Nazi Party.

(iii) Produced in 1929, this was a plan by which German reparations would be paid over a period of 58½ years; it also reduced the cost of reparations to about a quarter of the figure originally demanded in 1921.

With one mark for each question, these one-sentence answers should be quite enough to gain those marks. There is no need to write more.

■ (b) (i) Document I states that the German Social Democratic Party was 'essentially conservative' and was unlikely to appeal to those who 'believed that a thorough change in economic conditions was necessary'. 'Another section of German youth ... wanted a German revolution, a German Socialism.'

Document II states that 'radicalism combined with nationalism exercises a powerful fascination on young voters who are bored with German party politics ... [and] ... find the Socialists too dull'. These young voters had a 'hatred of wealth and privilege' and found capitalists partly responsible for the national malaise (line 21); they might normally have been expected to support the SPD.

(ii) Document I states that communism was seen by some German youth as 'Russian', 'cruel', 'unindividual' and 'anti-national' – they wanted a social revolution which would be 'national'.

Document II claims that young voters found the Communists 'too sectarian and Russian' but would be willing to support a party that combined radicalism with nationalism (line 17).

Both documents give broadly similar reasons for the rejection of the two parties; the desire for a '*national* and *socialist* revolution', as promised by Hitler, was obviously the key.

■ (c) Document I shows the positive attractions of Nazism as the promise of a social revolution which would be 'national', the promise of a strong Reich to overcome the humiliation of the Treaty of Versailles, the promise of a future with 'jobs, recovery, a new national honour', and for active supporters who would fight in the SA, 'three marks a day, food, uniforms, and an adventurous life'.

Document II stresses, firstly, the 'tremendous energy', 'strong emotions' and 'novel appeal' of the Nazi Party and the 'immense exaltation' of their campaigning; secondly, the 'powerful fascination' for young voters of 'radicalism combined with nationalism'; lastly the focusing of discontent on such scapegoats as the 'Jews, the Young Plan, the capitalists, the Stock Exchange.'

■ (d) The whole tone of this document is deeply hostile towards the Nazis. The division of the country between the minority ('Hitlerites and Hugenberg Nationalists') and the majority 'which embraces practically all other parties' is deplored, as is the 'arbitrary decision of the President' (the appointment of Hitler as Chancellor) which puts the minority in control of the majority. Rumbold states that 'the entire intelligentsia of the country' (and gives an odd list of those he means, lines 24–6) and 'moderate and reasonable people in all ranks' are ranged against this minority. There is no doubt that his sympathies lie with the 'majority' rather than the 'minority', which he criticises for their immaturity, ignorance and gullibility. There can be no doubt of his hostility to the Nazis: the use of emotive phrases ('unprecedented fashion', 'arbitrary decision') and the comparison between the 'moderate and reasonable people of all ranks' and the youth who are 'immature', 'ignorant' and prey to 'unscrupulous demagogues' clearly reveal his prejudices.

> **'Language and tone' questions** *often turn up. Quote as much as possible when answering them, normally by giving the actual words used in the document. Remember that most document questions are like detective stories: the documents contain clues which you must find to answer those questions. Try to make sure that you don't miss any of them; examiners often criticise candidates who have done so and thus lost marks which can only be given for finding them.*

■ **(e)** Document I, from *The Nation*, an American political periodical, possibly influenced by the prevailing ideas of the 'New Deal', appears to look kindly upon the Nazis' intended 'social revolution'. Opposition to 'Russian' communism might well be applauded by such a source, while Nazi Germany appeared at its most respectable in the year of the Berlin Olympics. The content appears to be accurate in its comments on the support Hitler gained from young people.

Document II, from *The New Statesman*, comments on the results of the 1930 Reichstag elections. Admiration for the Nazis comes oddly from a British socialist periodical and can only be explained by a belief in the 'socialism' of the NSDAP and perhaps also by admiration for the success of their campaign which had given the Nazis their first political breakthrough. Attacks on capitalists and the Stock Exchange would also have been popular with *The New Statesman*. Altogether, the analysis of the situation seems as accurate as it could be in the 1930s.

Document III shows the British Ambassador's reaction to Hitler's appointment as Chancellor (January 1933). The 'majority' he describes may well have been generally opposed to the Nazis at this time (although there were certain glaring exceptions), but their number must be compared to the 'millions of immature young men and women' (certainly not the only Nazi supporters) who had voted for the NSDAP in November 1932, giving them a total of nearly 11.5 million votes.

While the authors of Documents I and II may show some pro-Nazi bias, Rumbold is more strongly biased the other way, and obviously inaccurate in assessing Nazi support, particularly from the lower middle class.

> *You may have noticed that these answers are longer than the others – in fact, by about 50 words. It should be quite possible to save that amount by rewriting some of the answers without losing any of their content. You should try it, because one of the chief causes of bad marks in* **document questions** *is that candidates are unable to say what they want in a short enough space to allow them to answer all questions in the time allowed.*

The Enabling Act

■ (a) The new Nazi policy of achieving its aims 'with constitutional means' was worked out by Hitler in Landsberg after the failed Munich Putsch of 1923 – 'instead of working to achieve power by armed conspiracy, we shall have to hold our noses and enter the Reichstag'. Success in the 1930 election seemed at last to have justified this policy when Hitler spoke in the trial at Leipzig. In his defence of the pro-Nazi officers, he was careful to distinguish means from ends: the means were to be within the constitution (lines 1–2); the end was to be 'a state ... that corresponds to our ideas'. The chairman of the court accepted his argument (lines 5–6).

Another set of questions on **prescribed texts**, *with no easy marks to be gained on simple* **definition questions**. *You should also be ready to use your own knowledge in the answers, particularly if it's based on other prescribed documents.*

■ (b) In the Reichstag elections of 5 March 1933, the last to be held according to the Weimar Constitution, 'violence and terror dominated' (Lynch) while the people's fears, both present and future, were played on in Nazi propaganda, paid for by big donations from commerce and industry. Although the Nazis won 288 seats and their coalition with the Nationalists had a bare overall majority of 51.7%, this was well short of the two-thirds majority required to pass an Enabling Act. Nevertheless, Hitler claimed that a 'revolution had taken place' in Germany and that 'ultimately Marxism would no longer exist' there.

You could well claim that this answer does not do what is required – which is to say why Hitler regarded the events of 5 March 1933 as a 'revolution'. After analysing a document and adding facts from your own knowledge it is very easy to forget exactly what the question asked.

On the day of the announcement of the election results, which didn't give the Nazi Party the two-thirds majority it had expected, it's not surprising that Hitler should seek to impress the Cabinet, which still contained non-Nazi members, with the extent of his victory. He could well see the result as a 'revolution' if he was convinced by Goering's plan that the passing of an Enabling Act was now possible.

■ (c) In Document II, Hitler claimed that the imprisonment of 'the deputies of the German Communist Party' (as a result of the Decree for the Protection of People and State signed by Hindenburg on the day after the Reichstag fire) would enable a two-thirds majority for an Enabling Law to be obtained in the Reichstag. Goering proposed an equally undemocratic means by which deputies who absented themselves from the session to prevent a two-thirds quorum would suffer financially (lines 13–15). In Document III, the presence of the SA and SS 'along the walls of the hall' was obviously intimidatory, as were the reports of arrests and beatings which had reached the SPD members.

The arrest of the Communist deputies after the Reichstag fire was legalised by the decree referred to above. Goering's proposal to prevent deputies absenting themselves may well have been legal if he was empowered to 'change the rules'. It does not seem as if the presence of the SA and SS on the floor of the Kroll Opera House was illegal. Thus all the actions described in Documents II and III appear to show Hitler abiding by his pledge of legality while authorising extremely anti-democratic actions.

Exercise 7

■ (d) Hitler states, in Document I: 'In this constitutional way we shall try to gain decisive majorities in the legislative bodies'. This intention was followed in passing the Enabling Act, which was then used to 'give the state the form that corresponds to our ideas'. Document III indicates the sort of pressure that could be legally applied to opposition deputies, but it did not prevent the SDP members voting against the Enabling Act.

The Nazis thus needed the votes of the Centre Party to achieve their two-thirds majority. Hitler promised in a speech (23 March 1933) 'to respect the rights of the Catholic Church and to uphold religious and moral values' (Lynch). In addition, the Centre were intimidated by threats to remove Catholic civil servants from office. Lay Catholics and the Church authorities were satisfied with Hitler's promises and even the distinguished historian of the party could convince himself that it would be possible to co-operate with, and even influence, the NSDAP.

Thus the ease with which the Enabling Act was eventually passed (444 to 94) resulted from the legal 'persuasion' of the Centre Party to give its support rather than from the unsuccessful intimidation of the SDP.

■ (e) The Enabling Act has been described as giving 'the destruction of parliamentary democracy the appearance of legality' (Noakes and Pridham) and as 'the constitutional foundation stone of the Third Reich' (Lynch). *Gleichschaltung* (co-ordination) could now begin, a combined operation from above and below, aimed at destroying German federalism, the trade unions and all other political parties. Laws of 31 March 1933 and 7 April 1933 ensured the Nazi Party a majority in all state assemblies and appointed Reich Governors for each state. On 2 May 1933, all German workers' organisations were merged into DAF (the German Labour Front) and the power of the trade unions was broken. The Communist Party had been proscribed after the Reichstag fire, the SDP was banned on 22 June 1933, all other parties dissolved themselves and the Nazi Party was declared the only legal party in the Reich (14 July 1933). This political revolution came partly from the power now enjoyed by the SA at the local level – 'a revolution from below' – but it was also dictated by party leaders from Berlin – 'a revolution from above' – using the Enabling Act to provide the typical legislation of the Third Reich – government laws and Führer edicts. Thus the aim of the Nazi movement was realised.

Exercise 8

The 'Night of the Long Knives' and its consequences

■ **(a) (i)** Ernst Röhm, one of Hitler's earliest supporters and leader of the SA, was shot in the purge of 30 June 1934.

(ii) The SA was the paramilitary wing of the Nazi Party. Its members tended to represent the populist, anti-capitalist, left wing of the party.

> *Once again, these **definition** answers should be quite enough to gain two marks. The second sentence in (ii) has been included because it's an important point in the answers to other questions.*

■ **(b)** In Document I, Röhm may be included among those 'whom Hitler had lauded to the skies'. Document II identifies Röhm, the SA and the left wing as those who were diverging, in views and policy, from Hitler, the army and the right wing. Dodd, in Document III, identifies Röhm as one who believed 'a second more radical revolution was necessary'; his 'elimination' indicates a temporary diminution of the 'strength of the radicals'.

■ **(c) (i)** Laski, in Document I, refers to the supposed 'conspiracy' (line 3) which was the reason given by Hitler for the execution of the conspirators. Document II extends the description of this conspiracy as a 'Schleicher–Röhm plot' and indicates that 'the purge ... was precipitated by the decision of Röhm and Schleicher to launch a *coup d'état*'.

(ii) Laski complains, in Document I, that 'so far not a scrap of evidence has been produced to prove a conspiracy'. He goes on to state that 'the whole thing bears all the marks of tyranny' and claims (lines 7–10) that 'murder upon the basis of conspiracy' and 'execution on suspicion' are a popular solution employed by tyrants to deal with discontent.

Sargent, in Document II , voices his 'disbelief in the existence of a Schleicher–Röhm plot' and finds no evidence for an impending *coup d'état*.

Thus neither writer accepts Hitler's explanation.

> *These answers are, in total, about **twenty** words longer than is usual. You might well consider that the second sentence in answer (c)(i) might be severely pruned in order to save this amount of words.*

■ **(d)** Document I is an extract from an article by Harold Laski, a left-wing socialist academic, writing in *The Daily Herald*, the 1930s tabloid, financed by the trade unions. The language is such as might appeal to his readers: 'grisly events ... mutterings of discontent ... get nerves ...'. But the whole tone is much more strongly anti-Nazi than the other documents – as might be expected from a British socialist in the mid-1930s.

Documents II and III are both written by diplomats, and are official papers. Sargent coolly analyses the 'growing divergence of views and policy' within the Nazi government, declines to believe in a conspiracy without evidence and stresses (lines 18–20) the importance of the consequences rather than the events themselves. Dodd sees Röhm as a believer in 'a second more radical revolution' and also stresses the likely consequences.

Thus Laski concentrates on illustrating the tyranny of Nazi rule, the diplomats on possible changes in Germany's future policy.

Another **'language and tone'** *question. A comparison between an article in a tabloid paper and two diplomatic papers isn't too difficult to write. The accent on the present situation in the first document and on changes in future policy in the second is worth remembering for the future.*

■ (e) The origins of the three documents are described above (answer (d)). Laski's article in *The Daily Herald* would be useful to the historian as an indication of how the British left was already painting Hitler as a tyrant after he had made Germany a one-party state, emasculated the trade unions and thrown many socialists and communists into concentration camps.

Sargent's comments on the Ambassador's despatch indicate that some members of the British Foreign Office were unsympathetic towards Nazi Germany and unwilling to believe in a conspiracy which seems to have been accepted by the Ambassador. They also indicate that Sargent has recognised the importance of the position of the army in Hitler's Germany.

Dodd shows that the American Ambassador has correctly seen Röhm as a radical Nazi supporting a 'second revolution' and that 'his elimination' would be 'a stern lesson in party discipline' to any who might wish to oppose Hitler in the future. He also provides a typically optimistic scenario for the future (lines 22–5).

■ (f) Sargent sees 'the emergence of the army as the dominant force in Germany today' as the most importance consequence of the purge.

Dodd forecasts a *temporary* lessening of radical strength and a consequential increase in the importance of 'the conservative elements which desire a more liberal domestic and foreign policy with eventual monarchist leanings'. He also finds the purge to be 'primarily a stern lesson in party discipline'.

Both predictions were partly inaccurate. Sargent was correct in viewing these events as a final defeat for the left wing and the SA. But he was wrong to see the army as the 'dominant force in Germany' in the future; Hitler was determined to build up its power purely to make his foreign policy aims possible, with himself as the all powerful commander-in-chief.

Dodd was correct in his view that the purge would ensure party discipline – no opponent like Röhm was to emerge in the future. However, 'conservative elements' were never able to provide a 'more liberal domestic and foreign policy', or a return to the monarchy.

Both diplomats underestimated Hitler's powers as Führer and the obsession with which he would pursue his goals.

Both diplomatic observers tend to view the situation in old left-wing/right-wing terms, without realising that Hitler's Nazi dictatorship provided a new, third force within Germany.

Economic problems in the Third Reich

■ (a) The 'New Plan' was introduced by Schacht (appointed Economics Minister, 2 May 1934) in September 1934 in order to deal with the foreign exchange crisis. In 1934 Germany's balance of payments showed a deficit of 284 million RM. As Noakes and Pridham have shown, this was 'essentially the result of two separate developments: firstly, the large raw material imports required by the rearmament and work creation programmes; secondly, the high value of the German Mark which made German exports too expensive. By mid-June 1934 Germany's gold and foreign exchange reserves had fallen to 100 million RM and emergency action was essential. The Reichsbank was 'forced to allocate foreign exchange on a day-to-day basis, giving out no more foreign exchange than it received'; Schacht was appointed and produced his 'New Plan' including 'an absolute moratorium on Germany's foreign debts ... [and] ... the regulation of imports through government supervision of the allocation of foreign exchange'.

> *Questions on prescribed texts will tend to be more detailed compared with those on* **'unseen'** *documents and will also demand more knowledge of other documents in the collection. Questions will often be* **factual**, *as in* **(a)**, **(b)** *and* **(d)**; *or require considerable knowledge of events beyond the topic of the documents in the question, as in* **(c)** *and* **(e)**.

■ (b) Before 1933 the German workers had largely remained loyal to the SPD and the communists. After they had seized power, the Nazis were determined to eliminate the hostile trade unions and win the workers' support for their new state. The free trade unions were destroyed (2 May 1933) and the German Labour Front (DAF) was created (6 May 1933). The NSBO, 'which had attempted to provide a Nazi alternative to the trade unions', became subordinate to the DAF, which was to incorporate employers as well as workers and to be, in Hitler's words, an 'honest broker' between the classes which would bring class warfare to an end. Organised 'both regionally and according to branches of industry, trade and commerce' and under the leadership of the ambitious Dr Ley, the DAF's income was eventually three times greater than the party's and it acquired a large business empire, as well as control over the 'Beauty of Labour' and 'Strength through Joy' movements. Vocational training was another inevitable responsibility.

> **Exact dates** *given in brackets are not to be learnt by heart and reproduced in the exam; they are there for reference.*

■ (c) The New Plan represented a 'far more comprehensive and detailed application of [the] principles of exchange control and import regulation than had previously existed'. The government could now control both the kind and the source of imports (lines 2–4) while bilateral trade agreements became easier, including barter arrangements (lines 5–8). Thus the New Plan illustrates a change in economic focus (compared with that before 1933) by which strict government control enabled foreign trade to secure the political goals of rearmament and economic self-sufficiency and the economic penetration of south-east Europe.

The Four-Year Plan (line 14) which replaced Schacht's policy in 1936, called for the German economy to be fit for war within four years. One of the priorities highlighted in the plan was vocational training (lines 13–15), which was to overcome the shortage of skilled labour.

The Four-Year Plan thus represents an even clearer change in Nazi economic focus.

■ (d) There is general agreement that Germany did not, by 1939, possess a war economy and thus the Four-Year Plan had failed to achieve its goal. Its success, in fact, was mixed. The production of synthetic oil and rubber was well below the targets set, although the production of aluminium and explosives was greatly expanded. However, 'Germany's reliance on imports had not been exacerbated further ... [while] ... German industrial production had increased by 105% since 1935' (Layton). But despite the Four-Year Plan, 'the German economy had been subject to no more than partial mobilisation'; it could not provide both guns and butter. However, the Nazis had succeeded in carrying out a massive rearmament programme without 'either a wages explosion or serious price inflation and above all without mass opposition'.

> *It is even more important not to have to include long quotations in answers to* **document questions**. *In the answer to* **Question (d)**, *it's possible to commit the quotation from Layton to memory, but the second and third unattributed quotations should be expressed in your own words.*
> *Generally speaking, you should only quote in full those quotations whose author you can give, thus the important summing-up of the Four-Year Plan in the answer to* **Question (e)** *should be in your own words, or certainly in those which do not have quotation marks.*

■ (e) Documents I and II give a restricted view of the economic problems facing the Third Reich. Document I refers to 'the decline in German exports' (without revealing its chief cause in the overvalued Reichmark) and 'the consequent decline in foreign exchange receipts' (leading to the foreign exchange crisis which the New Plan tried to solve). 'Barter transactions' are one answer (lines 5–8) but the whole emphasis is on the necessity for the strict control of imports (which were needed for the rearmament programme). Section 4 refers to bilateral trade agreements which were a necessary feature of Nazi foreign policy.

Document II refers to 'the current shortage of skilled workers' which was hampering the rearmament programme from 1936 onwards. The Four-Year Plan had only limited success in its aim of mobilising the German economy for war in 1939, for it was never 'a comprehensive and well-coordinated plan ... [and] ... Germany was still dependent on foreign sources of supply for one third of her raw material requirements' by 1939.

It is hardly surprising that two official documents do not admit that the German economy was overloaded; it could not sustain a simultaneous pursuit of guns, butter and massive building projects.

The Hossbach Memorandum

■ **(a) (i)** Hitler's reference to the 'racial community' is to the somewhat vague concept of *Volksgemeinschaft* in the Nazi ideology. It meant 'working together for the benefit of the nation; the provision of jobs and social benefits; and the encouragement of "German values"' (Layton). Here Hitler is stressing its racial aspect: only members of the German *Volk* could participate and these were, by definition, members of the Aryan race.

    (ii) *Lebensraum* (living space) for the German people was one of Hitler's constant demands. Territorial expansion into eastern Europe would provide raw materials, cheap labour and the destruction of Soviet communism. It would involve the establishment of a *Reich* (empire) to include all members of the *Volk* and then further expansion into Soviet territory. Only thus could Germany become a superpower, able to compete with, and eventually challenge, the British Empire and the USA.

> *Once again, we can see a difference in the questions set when prescribed texts are being examined. There are* **six** *marks given for these two* **definition questions** *and they demand a knowledge of both topics which is beyond the subject of these documents.*

■ **(b)** During the summer and autumn of 1936, all three of Germany's armed forces began to compete for limited economic resources (raw materials and skilled labour) in order to be ready for war in 1940, as envisaged in the Four-Year Plan. The navy's programme, in particular, was subject to growing delays by the summer of 1937, and Admiral Raeder wrote in desperation to Blomberg to suggest that Hitler should decide on the 'general conflict over priorities in the allocation of raw materials and labour' between the services. Hitler summoned a meeting between the service heads and the Foreign Minister on 5 November 1937, and decided to use the occasion for a major speech on the international situation and future German foreign policy. Document I is an excerpt from that speech as reported by Colonel Hossbach.

> **Questions (b) and (e)** *are factual questions which again can only be answered by reference to knowledge outside the scope of these documents on the* **Hossbach Memorandum**.

■ **(c)** Hitler's plans revolve around the problem of obtaining *Lebensraum* for the German people in Europe rather than overseas; moreover, the problem must be solved by 1943–5 while Germany still enjoyed superiority in armaments. Hitler concentrated on the simultaneous overthrow of Czechoslovakia and Austria. He stated that the 'necessity for action might arise before 1943–5' if either (1) there was civil war in France or (2) France became engaged in war with another country. If either event occurred, the opportunity to move against Austria and Czechoslovakia must be seized, 'even as early as 1938'.

The Wehrmacht were happy to approve moves against Austria and Czechoslovakia but disagreed with Hitler about the risks involved. Thus, in Document II, Jodl at first insists on 'complete preparedness for war in all spheres' before an attack on Czechoslovakia, states that 'Operation Green' may have to be 'postponed for years' until the time is ripe, and concentrates more on Britain's role (lines 13–18) rather than that of France. Plans might be drawn up for an offensive (Operation Green) rather than a defensive war (Operation Red) against Czechoslovakia, but Blomberg and Fritsch were doubtful whether Britain and France had 'written off the Czechs'.

*The answer to **Question (c)** requires a much fuller knowledge of Hitler's speech at the meeting than is given in **Document I**. Where documents are presented '**unseen**', this sort of question would be almost impossible. Similarly, in **Document II**, you need to know the difference between 'Operation Green' and 'Operation Red' and to understand the different weight given to dangers of opposition from Britain and France by Hitler and the German army.*

(d) Bullock observes that 'the winter of 1937–38 thus marks a beginning and an end'; a beginning in that Hitler now believed that German rearmament had progressed far enough to take the risks involved in moving to the second stage of his plan, 'the creation of a Greater Germany, opening the way ultimately to the east'. Although the threat of force involved greater risk, he still hoped to achieve his immediate objectives by diplomacy. This winter also marked the end of the alliance with the traditional German élites (represented by Blomberg, Fritsch, Neurath and Schacht) who could now be dispensed with in favour of more pliable Nazis.

These documents give little indication of these important changes: *Lebensraum* and a Greater German Reich were not new concepts (lines 6–7) and although Document II shows Jodl unwillingly admitting that 'Operation Green' might have to 'start before the completion of Germany's full preparedness for war', it hardly indicates Hitler's willingness to run new risks and the Wehrmacht's response to that situation. But he does declare that Document I should be regarded as 'his last will and testament'.

*'**How useful ...?**' questions are common in papers on prescribed texts. Make sure you know how to answer them. They obviously require considerable knowledge beyond the topic of the documents in the question.*

(e) The first reason for controversy over the Hossbach Memorandum is that it is 'a copy of a copy, the original as well as the first copy of which are missing'. There is also doubt as to whether it is based on memory or on notes; it was certainly written five days after the conference. A document of such uncertain provenance would not normally have excited so much attention; the fact that it was used as evidence at the Nuremberg trials for Hitler's 'irrevocable decision to go to war' has given it great importance in the debate between 'Intentionalists' and 'Structuralists'. For the former, the memorandum is important evidence for Hitler being 'an ideological visionary with a programme for aggression' (Kershaw); the latter have dismissed it as 'simply a manoeuvre in domestic affairs to overcome the conservatives' doubts about the pace of rearmament' (Layton). The controversy continues.

*Discussion on the controversy surrounding the **Hossbach Memorandum** is briefly introduced in **Noakes and Pridham**, Nazism 1919–1945, **Vol 3, page 680**. Further details may be found in **Layton, Williamson** and **Kershaw**. Its importance in the 'Intentionalists' v 'Structuralists' debate is obvious; you must be familiar with the details if you're to write well on the broader aspects of Nazi foreign policy.*